Retirement in Perspective

How to Make Sure Your Retirement Plan Reveals a Purpose

BOB HORNE, RICP®
NuVenture Financial Group

Bob Horne/NuVenture Financial Group
13241 Bartram Park Blvd., Suite 913
Jacksonville, FL 32258
nuventurefinancialgroup.com

Book layout ©2022 Advisors Excel, LLC

Retirement in Perspective/Bob Horne.
ISBN 9798876130174

"You can change lives . . . Act like it."

~ Joel Johnson, Managing Partner
Johnson Brunetti Retirement & Investment Specialists[1]

Somehow, by the grace of God, I found my way to where I am right now in my life. Through imperfect and difficult times, He always knew where I was headed—even when I didn't. I give all the glory to my Lord and Savior, Jesus Christ.

Table of Contents

The Importance of Planning

One downward trend determined the fate of my career, and I could see it coming.

As the branch manager of a bank, I noticed exactly how much in assets my parent company hemorrhaged. I read the reports each day. Lines that once reflected consistent revenue became awash in red ink.

Within the broad corporate structure of the bank, action became necessary. Payroll had to be cut. It was only a matter of when. The financial crisis of what would come to be known as the Great Recession was real.

The date was February 12, 2009. Some of us learn in school that it's Abraham Lincoln's birthday. In conjunction with George Washington's birthday, our country observes a federal holiday to mark the significance of those iconic statesmen. Unfortunately, the Monday I had been dreading proved anything but celebratory after I learned of my bank termination in an email.

A couple of weeks later, I had an epiphany of sorts. I finished mowing my lawn and as I waited for the water in the shower to warm up, my mind raced. I knew I must make a career decision.

I could ride out the financial crisis knowing I could probably become a branch manager of a bank again. The money would be decent, the job reasonably secure, my family comfortable, and my lifestyle conventional.

But as steam began rising from the shower, the water sufficiently hot, it dawned on me. I would be miserable if I returned to a bank, again shackled to corporate policies that robbed me of any freedom to fully help people with their financial needs.

I didn't need to think long and hard about other positions in the financial industry. The prospect of becoming a financial advisor had intrigued me before. While I wasn't quite sure about what opportunities I could pursue, I knew I could obtain the proper licensing and possessed confidence that I could excel at a new job.

I had done so before with other companies. It's about grit. Learn from mistakes by dusting yourself off and focus on individual growth. Banking could be my fallback, sure. Moreover, it would be my motivation to never return to that industry.

Opportunities arose, but financial sacrifices had to be made, in part, because the fallout from the Great Recession proved difficult. Financial setbacks made times difficult for many, and I was right alongside those I began to see as clients. I drained my 401(k) account attempting to resurrect my career—a consideration I would never recommend.

Yet in the years since facing those dark times, I realize the frightening ordeal of being a banker attempting to overcome an American banking crisis made me the professional I am today—a financial advisor who oversees his own company, NuVenture Financial Group.

All things happen for a reason. I believe wholeheartedly in that. I am aware of watershed moments, including the precise time I decided to pursue my own financial advisory practice. Correction: financial advisory business.

After working for a couple of advisors after leaving the banking industry, beginning by making cold calls while attempting to secure leads selling life insurance, I continually wanted to pursue something more robust and meaningful. I frequently pondered new ideas. My ambitions, however, could sometimes be met with pushbacks.

Until one day, I sensed I was in the position to push back myself.

Yet another proposal was met by a patented response from the owner, saying, "We've never done it that way before." With that, my idea got scratched. Resistance to change can be real, and perhaps understandable to an extent, but it can also stifle the growth of a team and a company.

I left that meeting, went directly to Chris Morrison's office, and shut the door. We had become close friends in the same office and talked extensively about opening a financial advisory business. I told him it was time. I wanted to make the move.

That was in March 2018. In January 2019, we opened NuVenture Financial Group, where I serve as CEO and President. Chris serves as Vice President.

Since opening the firm, I have found it imperative not to stifle original thought. I tell everyone that NuVenture is a small business. There is no red tape. I want to experiment and be willing to take calculated, reasonable risks that can potentially streamline processes and boost production while constantly keeping the needs of clients our top priority.

I pinch myself sometimes, knowing that important decisions rest with me, yet include open and active input from everyone on our staff.

Frankly, February 12, 2009, was a day that changed my life. But it also made me a better financial professional—one who can thoroughly examine the retirement needs of families who become NuVenture clients.

My hand was forced by my termination. Thousands in the banking sector lost their jobs, beginning with the 2007 onset of the financial crisis.[2] Had that economic downturn not transpired, however, I may have been content to remain in the banking industry.

Believe me, the hardships presented some real-life difficulties. My wife, April, homeschooled our children, and while that is a full-time task, it does not generate income.

---

[2] Michael J. de la Merced. The New York Times. December 11, 2008.
"Bank of America to Cut 35,000 Jobs Over 3 Years"
https://www.nytimes.com/2008/12/12/business/12bank.html#:

Nonetheless, I committed to sticking it out with professional opportunities I accepted. I knew it was my destiny to remain in the financial industry and eventually find ways to help clients with any planning issues.

I did not have an option to fail. My efforts hardened my resolve and forged me into the man I am now—committed to family, faith, and the vitality of NuVenture Financial Group, a business concerned with looking out for the financial well-being of our clients.

Potential Risks to Your Ideal Retirement

Ever feel like life gets in the way and prevents you from doing things you should not ignore? I think if we're honest with ourselves, we've all put off obligations we know are important.

In your case, you may be reading this book because it's time to get serious about financial planning and, specifically, devising a way to best prepare for retirement. A retirement plan should be based on more components than just your investments or your finances. The preparation of that strategy begins with your desires, ambitions, and goals for this fulfilling season of life.

There's no such thing as a silly question. Not when one of the most common questions we hear from folks regarding retirement is, "Am I going to be okay?" Often, it seems, people are reluctant to meet with financial professionals because they worry they might sound uneducated. Yet, it's understandable for you to be a novice when it comes to financial issues and retirement concerns. You've been busy with your lives and your careers. Time spent away from work has meant time spent being around those you love and engaging in the activities you enjoy. Retirement provides the opportunity to do even more of that, while not fretting over work obligations.

Concerns people have about what they may encounter during retirement can be far-reaching and still perfectly legitimate. For a quick snapshot, I want to provide a brief sampling of wide-ranging issues that can come up during discussions about what to potentially brace for in retirement. This book will touch on many of these issues in further detail.

Politics: A presidential election often stirs emotions regarding potential effects on the economy. Investors grow anxious about how a new president can influence market returns. It's Congress, however, that establishes tax laws and passes spending bills. Yet the president can indirectly affect the economy and the stock market in various ways such as the appointment of policymakers, development of international relations, and influential sway on new legislation.

Taxes: An example of a president's influence can be cited in signature legislation passed during Donald Trump's presidency, the Tax Cuts and Jobs Act of 2017. However, our tax system remains progressive, so the more you earn, the higher the tax rate within each tax bracket of subsequently higher income. A thorough understanding of tax regulations can be crucial. A financial professional can help identify potential issues a tax professional can help solve.

Inflation: Government spending, which most recently spiked with relief packages designed to assist U.S. citizens during the COVID-19 pandemic, can fuel concerns of inflationary hikes stemming from an influx of money thrust at the same consumer goods. A retiree's income can be impacted by the effect inflation can have on a fixed budget. The value of currency decreases because inflation erodes purchasing power.

Health pandemic: The coronavirus outbreak could impact how Americans view risks and re-examine healthy habits. That, potentially, could be one of the effects of COVID-19 as we assess how long a pandemic can last and if others will occur in our lifetimes. The cost of health care can be surprising throughout retirement. It could become an issue people focus on even more following the pandemic, which had a particularly acute impact on some U.S. elder care facilities.

Cybersecurity: Think you'll give up your smartphone in retirement? No way, right? It's here to stay, along with other intellectual gadgetry, including devices that have not been patented or invented. Retirees are becoming more tech-savvy, yet they can also be more trusting, which can be problematic when responding to potential scammers by phone, text, or email. Cybercrime often uses technology to target potential victims. Scammers, much like technology, figure to only grow more sophisticated over time.

CHAPTER 1

Longevity

You would think the prospect of the grave would loom more frightening as we age, yet many retirees say their number one concern is actually running out of money in their twilight years.[3] This concern is, unfortunately, justified, in part, because of one significant factor: We're living longer.

According to the Social Security Administration's 2011 Trustee Report, in 1950, the average life expectancy for a sixty-five-year-old man was seventy-eight, and the average for a sixty-five-year-old woman was eighty-one. In the 2022 Trustees Report issued by the SSA, those averages were 81.94 and 84.66, respectively.[4]

The bottom line of many retirees' budget woes comes down to this: They just didn't plan to live so long. Now, when we are younger and in our working years, that's not something we necessarily see as a bad thing; don't some people fantasize about living forever or, at least, reaching the ripe old age of one hundred?

However, with a longer lifespan, as we near retirement, we face a few snags. Our resources are finite—we only have so much money to provide income—but our lifespans can be

---

3 Liz Weston. nerdwallet.com. March 25, 2021. "Will You Really Run Out of Money in Retirement?"
https://www.nerdwallet.com/article/finance/will-you-really-run-out-of-money-in-retirement
44 Social Security Administration. 2023 Trustees Report. "Actuarial Life Table" https://www.ssa.gov/oact/STATS/table4c6.html

unpredictably long, perhaps longer than our resources allow. Also, longer lives don't necessarily equate with healthier lives. The longer you live, the more money you will likely need to spend on health care, even excluding long-term care needs like nursing homes.

You will also run into inflation. If you don't plan to live another twenty-five years but end up doing so, inflation at an average 3 percent will approximately double the price of goods over that time period. Put a harsh twist on that and the buying power of a ninety-year-old will be half of what they possessed if they retired at sixty-five.[5]

Because we don't necessarily get to have our cake and eat it, too, our collective increased longevity hasn't necessarily increased the healthy years of our lives. Typically, our life-extending care most widely applies to the time in our lives when we will need more care in general. Think of common situations like a pacemaker at eighty-five, or cancer treatment at seventy-eight.

"Wow, Bob," I can hear you say. "Way to start with the good news first."

I know, I've painted a grim picture, but all I'm concerned about here is cost. It's hard to put a dollar sign on life, but that is essentially what we're talking about when discussing longevity and finances. Living longer isn't a bad thing; it just costs more, and one key to a sound retirement strategy is preparing for it in advance.

People are living longer and longer. Medical advancements have helped to prolong lifespans. This, naturally, affects our retirement planning. We must create retirement plans that account for the likelihood of greater longevity.

There are usually three distinct phases of retirement, each requiring its own set of strategies to ensure your entire retirement stays on course.

---

5 Bob Sullivan, Benjamin Curry. Forbes. April 28, 2021. "Inflation And Retirement Investments: What You Need to Know."
https://www.forbes.com/advisor/retirement/inflation-retirement-investments/

- **Stage One (the go-go years):** This stage is usually the first ten to fifteen years of retirement and will likely look like what you're doing now. You can travel and do all the things you've been wanting to accomplish. You usually still have your health, and this is the stage where you are likely to spend the most money. Good. We only have one life to live, so enjoy it!
- **Stage Two (the slow-go years):** In this stage, you may still have your health, but you may not have the energy to travel and do all the hobbies you once could. That's okay. There's still much to enjoy. Many of our families describe their perfect day as hanging around the house, gardening, reading, or being with family. These activities don't require a lot of exertion but are still very enjoyable.
- **Stage Three (the no-go years):** The Good Lord doesn't tell you the day you'll die. However, we all know it's going to happen. In this stage, estate planning, efficient family inheritance strategies, legacy planning, tax planning, and tactical Medicare (and Medicaid) planning are all likely to be important considerations. How do you make sure the wealth and resources you've accumulated over a lifetime aren't squandered in your last few years due to a lack of planning?

Living longer may be more expensive, but it can be so meaningful when you plan for your "just-in-cases."

Retiring Early

A key part of planning for retirement revolves around retirement income. After all, retirement is cutting the cord that tethers you to your employer—and your monthly check. However, that check often comes with many other benefits, particularly health care. Health care is often the thing that can unexpectedly put dreams for an early retirement on hold. Some employers offer health benefits to their retired workers, but that number has declined drastically over the past several decades. In 1988, among employers who offered health benefits to their workers, 66 percent offered health benefits to their retirees. In 2022, that number was 21 percent.[6]

So, with employer-offered retirement health benefits on the wane, this becomes a major concern for anyone looking to retire. This is particularly true for those looking to retire before age sixty-five, when they would become eligible for Medicare coverage. Fidelity estimates that the average retired couple at age sixty-five will need approximately $315,000 for health care expenses in retirement, not including long-term care.[7] Do you think it's likely that cost will decrease?

Even if you are working until age sixty-five or have plans to cover your health expenses until that point, I often have clients who incorrectly assume Medicare is their golden ticket to cover all expenses. That is simply not the case.

Retiring Later

Planning for a long life in retirement partly depends on when you retire. While many people end up retiring earlier than they anticipated—due to injuries, layoffs, family crises, and other unforeseen circumstances—continuing to work past age sixty (and even sixty-five) is still a viable option for others and can be an excellent way to help establish financial comfort in retirement.

There are many reasons for this. For one, you obviously still earn a paycheck and the benefits accompanying it. Medical coverage and beefing up your retirement accounts with further savings can be significant by themselves but continuing your

---

[6] Henry J. Kaiser Family Foundation. October 27, 2022. "2022 Employer Health Benefits Survey Section Eleven: Retiree Health Benefits." https://www.kff.org/report-section/ehbs-2022-section-11-retiree-health-benefits/

[7] Fidelity Viewpoints. Fidelity. August 29, 2022.. "How to Plan for Rising Health Care Costs." https://www.fidelity.com/viewpoints/personal-finance/plan-for-rising-health-care-costs

income also should keep you from dipping into your retirement funds, further allowing them the opportunity to grow.

Additionally, for many workers, their nine-to-five job is more than just clocking in and out. Having a sense of purpose can keep us active physically, mentally, and socially. That kind of activity and level of engagement may also help stave off many of the health problems that plague retirees. Avoiding a sedentary life is one of the advantages of staying plugged into the workforce, if possible.

Seminar attendees often pull me aside to ask if I can determine whether they have enough assets to retire and if so, can they retire at a desired age. Clearly, those become established goals for our team to recognize if those seminar attendees become clients. The goals translate into a clear mission for our team to determine if those new clients can hit their target date for retirement. My job is not only to help them achieve their goals, but inform them about ways it can be done.

I am obligated to tell them whether I believe they can retire at their desired age. Also, as their advisor, I must devise a Plan B if retirement must be put off a few years. Quite possibly, they may still need to work part-time for a few years, especially if they need income to cover health insurance costs if they leave full-time employment before reaching sixty-five, when they can sign up for Medicare.

Most clients hope to receive what we like to call their ***retirement permission slip.*** If continuing in the workforce is part of that equation, having that retirement permission slip in your back pocket can prove empowering. You're working, in part, because you want to be there. You like your job, the environment, and your co-workers. However, if the stress of work becomes too much, retirement is an option. When our team recognizes from analysis that retirement is attainable, we aim to give our clients the confidence to retire. This timeframe is a crucial period for aspiring retirees and accounts for the five-year periods before and after retirement. Sequence of return risk factors into any discussions regarding investments. You've reached the retirement caution zone.

Within the caution zone, however, precise execution helps avoid a harsh impact from market downturns, which can erode your retirement savings. Such an event could push back your desired retirement date. Also, after retirement, if someone peels money from their investments and the markets decline, it can create a snowball effect (sequence of return risk) that can harm the viability of your assets to account for your long-term income needs.

The retirement caution zone is a crucial component for retirees to navigate in order to cope favorably with elements related to longevity. Accumulation of assets is no longer the primary objective. Instead, the preservation of assets becomes paramount.

Health Care

Take a second to reflect on your health care plan. Although working up to or even past age sixty-five would allow you to avoid a coverage gap between your working years and Medicare, that may not be an option for you. Even if it is, when you retire, you will need to make some decisions about what kind of insurance coverage you may need to supplement your Medicare. Are there any medical needs you have that may require coverage in addition to Medicare? Did your parents or grandparents have any inherited medical conditions you might consider using a special savings plan to cover?

These are all questions that are important to review with your financial professional so you can be sure you have enough money put aside for health care.

Long-Term Care

Longevity means the need for long-term care is statistically more likely to happen. If you intend to pass on a legacy, planning for long-term care is paramount, since most estimates project nearly 70 percent of Americans will need some type of it.[8] However, this may be one of the biggest, most stressful pieces of longevity planning I encounter in my work. For one thing, who wants to talk about the point in their lives when they may feel the most limited? Who wants to dwell on what will happen if they no longer can toilet, bathe, dress, or feed themselves?

I get it; this is a less-than-fun part of planning. But a little bit of preparation now can go a long way!

When it comes to your longevity, just like with your goals, one of the important things to do is sit and dream. It may not be the fun, road-trip-to-the-Grand-Canyon kind of dreaming, but you can spend time envisioning how you want your twilight years to look.

For instance, if it is important for you to live in your home for as long as possible, who will provide for the day-to-day fixes and to-dos of housework if you become ill? Will you set aside money for a service, or do you have relatives or friends nearby whom you could comfortably allow to help you? Do you prefer in-home care over a nursing home or assisted living? This could be a good time to discuss the possibility of moving into a retirement community versus staying where you are or whether it's worth moving to another state and leaving relatives behind.

These are all important factors to discuss with your spouse and children, as *now* is the right time to address questions and concerns. For instance, is aging in place more important to one spouse than the other? Are the friends or relatives who live nearby emotionally, physically, and financially capable of helping you for a time if you face an illness?

Many families I meet find these conversations very uncomfortable, particularly when children discuss nursing home care with their parents. A knee-jerk reaction for many is to promise they will care for their aging parents. This is noble

---

8 Richard W. Johnson. urban.org. June 24, 2021. "What is the Lifetime Risk of Needing and Receiving Long-Term Services and Supports?" https://www.urban.org/research/publication/what-lifetime-risk-needing-and-receiving-long-term-services-and-supports

and well-intentioned, but there needs to be an element of realism here. Does "help" from an adult child mean they stop by and help you with laundry, cooking, home maintenance, and bills? Or does it mean they move you into their spare room when you have hip surgery? Are they prepared to help you use the restroom and bathe if that becomes difficult for you to do on your own?

I don't mean to discourage families from caring for their own; this can be a profoundly admirable relationship when it works out. However, I've seen families put off planning for late-in-life care based on a tenuous promise that the adult children would care for their parents, only to watch as the support system crumbles. Sometimes this is because the assumed caregiver hasn't given serious thought to the preparation they would need, both in a formal sense and regarding their personal physical, emotional, and financial commitments. This is often also because we can't see the future: Alzheimer's disease and other maladies of old age can exact a heavy toll. When a loved one reaches the point where he or she is at risk of wandering away or needs help with two or more activities of daily living, it can be more than one person or family can realistically handle.

If you know what you want, communicate with your family about both the best-case and worst-case scenarios. Then, hope for the best, and plan for the worst.

Realistic Cost of Care

Wrapped up in your planning should be a consideration for the cost of long-term care. The potential costs for such care and treatment can be underestimated, especially by those who have maintained robust health and find it difficult to envision future declines to their condition.

Another piece of planning for long-term care costs is anticipating inflation. It's common knowledge that prices have been and keep rising, which will lower your purchasing power on everything from food to medical care. Long-term care is a big piece of the inflation-disparity pie.

While local costs vary from state to state, the following table shows the national median for various forms of long-term care (plus projections that account for a 3 percent annual inflation, so you can see what I am referencing):[9]

Long-Term Care Costs: Inflation				
	Informal Care	Home Care	Assisted Living	Nursing Home (semi-private room)
Annual 2024	$42,037	$33,621	$60,874	$113,522
Annual 2034	$56,495	$45,184	$81,810	$160,134
Annual 2044	$75,924	$60,723	$109,945	$225,884
Annual 2054	$102,036	$81,607	$147,757	$318,632

Fund Your Long-Term Care

One common mistake I see is those who haven't planned for long-term care because they assume the government will provide everything. But that's a big misconception. The government has two health insurance programs: Medicare and Medicaid. These can greatly assist you in your health care needs in retirement but usually don't provide enough coverage to cover all your health care costs in retirement. My firm isn't a government outpost, so we don't get to make decisions when it comes to forming policy and specifics about either one of these

---

9 Nationwide. 2022. "Compare Long-term Care costs from state to state" https://nationwidefinancialltcmap.hvsfinancial.com/ l

programs. I'm going to give an overview of both, but if you want to dive into the details of these programs, you can visit www.Medicare.gov and www.Medicaid.gov.

Medicare

Medicare covers those aged sixty-five and older and those who are disabled. Medicare's coverage of any nursing-home-related health issues is limited. It might cover your nursing home stay if it is not a "custodial" stay, and it isn't long-term. For example, if you break a bone or suffer a stroke, stay in a nursing home for rehabilitative care, and then return home, Medicare may cover you. But, if you have developed dementia or are looking to move to a nursing facility because you can no longer bathe, dress, toilet, feed yourself, or take care of your hygiene, etc., then Medicare is not going to pay for your nursing home costs.[10]

You can enroll in Medicare anytime during the three months before and three months after your sixty-fifth birthday. Miss your enrollment deadline, and you could risk paying increased premiums for the rest of your life.[11] On top of prompt enrollment, there are a few other things to think about when it comes to Medicare, not least among them being the need to understand the different "parts," what they do, and what they don't cover.

Part A

Medicare Part A is what you might think of as "classic" Medicare. Hospital care, some types of home health care, and major medical care fall under this. While most enrollees pay nothing for this service (as they likely paid into the system for at least ten years), you may end up paying, either based on work

---

[10] Medicare.gov. "What Part A covers." https://www.medicare.gov/what-medicare-covers/part-a/what-part-a-covers.html

[11] Medicare.gov. "When can I sign up for Medicare?" https://www.medicare.gov/basics/get-started-with-medicare/sign-up/when-can-i-sign-up-for-medicare

history or delayed signup. In 2024, the highest premium is $505 per month, and a hospital stay does have a deductible — $1,632[12] And, if you have a hospital stay that surpasses sixty days, you could be looking at additional costs; keep in mind, Medicare doesn't pay for long-term care and services.

Part B

Medicare Part B is an essential piece of wrap-around coverage for Medicare Part A. It helps pay for doctor visits and outpatient services. This also comes with a price tag: Although the Part B annual deductible is only $240 in 2024, you will still pay 20 percent of all costs after that, with no limit on out-of-pocket expenses. The Part B monthly premium for 2024 ranges from the standard amount of $174.70 to $594.[13]

Part C

Medicare Part C, more commonly known as Medicare Advantage plans, are an alternative to a combination of Parts A, B, and sometimes D. Administered through private insurance companies, these have a variety of costs and restrictions, and they are subject to the specific policies and rules of the issuing carrier.

Part D

Medicare Part D is also through a private insurer and is supplemental to Parts A and B, as its primary purpose is to cover prescription drugs. Like any private insurance plan, Part D has its quirks and rules that vary from insurer to insurer.

---

[12] CMS.gov. October 12, 2023. "2024 Medicare Parts A & B Premiums and Deductibles" https://www.cms.gov/newsroom/fact-sheets/2024-medicare-parts-b-premiums-and-deductibles?ref=biztoc.com
[13] Ibid.

The Donut Hole

Even with a "Part D" in place, you may still have a coverage gap between what your Part D private drug insurance pays for your prescription and what basic Medicare pays. In 2024, the coverage gap is $5,030, meaning that after you meet your private prescription insurance limit, you will spend no more than 25 percent of your drug costs out-of-pocket before Medicare kicks in to pay for more prescription drugs.[14]

Note: In the donut hole, you pay up to 25 percent out of pocket for all covered medications. You leave the donut hole once you've spent $8,000 out of pocket for covered drugs in 2024, which is the last year for the donut hole. A $2,000 out-of-pocket cap takes effect for Medicare Part D in 2025.

Medicare Supplements

Medicare Supplement Insurance, MedSupp, Medigap, or plans labeled Medicare Part F, G, H, I, J . . . Known by a variety of monikers, this is just a fancy way of saying "medical coverage for those over sixty-five that picks up the tab for whatever the federal Medicare program(s) doesn't." Again, costs, limitations, etc., vary by carrier.

Does that sound like a bunch of government alphabet soup to you? It certainly does to me. Did you read the fine print? Unpredictable costs, varied restrictions, difficult-to-compare benefits, donut holes, and coverage gaps. That's par for the course with health care plans through the course of our adult lives. What gives? I thought Medicare was supposed to be easier, comprehensive, and at no cost!

The truth is there is probably no stage of life when health care is easy to understand.

---

[14] Medicare. "Costs in the coverage gap"
https://www.medicare.gov/drug-coverage-part-d/costs-for-medicare-drug-coverage/costs-in-the-coverage-gap

The best thing you can do for yourself is to scope out the health care field early, compare costs often, and prepare for out-of-pocket costs well in advance—decades, if possible.

Medicaid

Medicaid is a program the states administer, so funding, protocol, and limitations vary. Compared to Medicare, Medicaid more widely covers nursing home care, but it targets a different demographic: those with low incomes.

If you have more assets than the Medicaid limit in your state and need nursing home care, you will need to use those assets to pay for your care. You will also have a list of additional state-approved ways to spend some of these assets over the Medicaid limit, such as pre-purchasing burial plots and funeral expenses or paying off debts. After that, your remaining assets fund your nursing home stay until they are gone, at which point Medicaid will jump in.

Some people aren't stymied by this, thinking they will just pass on their financial assets early, gifting them to relatives, friends, and causes so they can qualify for Medicaid when they need it. However, to prevent this exact scenario, Uncle Sam has implemented the look-back period. Currently, if you enroll in Medicaid, you are subject to having the government scrutinize the last five years of your finances for large gifts or expenses that may subject you to penalties, temporarily making you ineligible for Medicaid coverage.

So, if you're planning to preserve your money for future generations and retain control of your financial resources during your lifetime, you'll probably want to prepare for the costs of longevity beyond a "government plan."

Self-Funding

One way to fund a longer life is the old-fashioned way, through self-funding. There are a variety of financial tools you can use, and they all have their pros and cons. If your assets are in low-interest financial vehicles (savings, bonds, CDs), you risk letting inflation erode the value of your dollar. Or, if you are relying on the stock market, you have more growth potential, but you'll also want to consider the possible implications of market volatility. What if your assets take a hit? If you suffer a loss in your retirement portfolio in early or mid-retirement, you might have the option to "tighten your belt," so to speak, and cut back on discretionary spending to allow your portfolio the room to bounce back. But, if you are retired and depend on income from a stock account that just hit a downward stride, what are you going to do?

HSAs

These days, you might also be able to self-fund through a health savings account, or HSA, if you have access to one through a high-deductible health plan (you will not qualify to save in an HSA after enrolling in Medicare). In an HSA, any growth of your tax-deductible contributions will be tax-free, and any distributions paid out for qualified health costs are also tax-free. Long-term care expenses count as health costs, so, if this is an option available to you, it is one way to use the tax advantages to self-fund your longevity. Bear in mind, if you are younger than sixty-five, any money you use for non-qualified expenses will be subject to taxes and penalties, and, if you are older than sixty-five, any HSA money you use for non-medical expenses is subject to income tax.

LTCI

One slightly more nuanced way to pay for longevity, specifically for long-term care, is long-term care insurance, or LTCI. As car insurance protects your assets in case of a car accident and home insurance protects your assets in case something happens to your house, long-term care insurance aims to protect your assets in case you need long-term care in an at-home or nursing home situation.

As with other types of insurance, you will pay a monthly or annual premium in exchange for an insurance company paying for long-term care down the road. Typically, policies cover two to three years of care, which is adequate for an "average" situation: it's estimated 70 percent of Americans will need about three years of long-term care of some kind.

Now, there are a few oft-cited components of LTCI that make it unattractive for some:

- Expense — LTCI can be expensive. It is generally less expensive the younger you are, but a sixty-five-year-old couple who purchased LTCI in 2023 could expect to pay a combined annual amount of $3,750 for a policy. And the annual cost only increases from there the older you are.[15]

- Limited options—Let's face it: LTCI may be expensive for consumers, but it can also be expensive for companies that offer it. With fewer companies willing to take on that expense, this narrows the market, meaning opportunities to price shop for policies with different options or custom benefits are limited.

- If you know you need it, you might not be able to get it—Insurance companies offering LTCI are taking on a risk that you may need LTCI. That risk is the foundation of the product—you may or may not need it. If you know you will need it because you have a dementia diagnosis or another illness for which you will need long-term care, you will likely not qualify for LTCI coverage.

- Use it or lose it—If you have LTCI and are in the minority of Americans who die having never needed long-term care, all the money you paid into your LTCI policy is gone.

- Possibly fluctuating rates—Your rate is not locked in on LTCI. Companies maintain the ability to raise or lower

---

[15] American Association for Long-Term Care Insurance. 2023. "Long-Term Care Insurance Facts – Data – Statistics – 2023 Reports" https://www.aaltci.org/long-term-care-insurance/learning-center/ltcfacts-2023.php

your premium amounts. This means some seniors face an ultimatum: Keep funding a policy at what might be a less affordable rate *or* lose coverage and let go of all the money they paid in so far.

After that, you might be thinking, "How can people possibly be interested in LTCI?" But let me repeat myself—it's anticipated that as many as 70 percent of Americans will need long-term care. And, although only one in ten Americans aged fifty-five-plus have purchased LTCI, keep in mind the high cost of nursing home care. Can you afford $7,000 a month to put into nursing home care and still have enough left over to protect your legacy? This is a very real concern considering one set of statistics reported a two-in-three chance that a senior citizen will become physically or cognitively impaired in their lifetime.[16] So, not to sound like a broken record, but it is vitally important to have a plan in place to deal with longevity and long-term care if you intend to leave a financial legacy.

Sadly, some of our clients, and even those who do not become clients after attending one of our events, will eventually move into an assisted living facility or require in-home medical care. So then, does that mean a long-term care insurance policy is essential to own?

Not always. The premiums in most long-term care insurance policies will most assuredly rise over time, which can be problematic for retirees on fixed incomes. Also, it's much like auto insurance. If you never have an accident, you're paying for a product you will never need. The same is true for long-term care insurance if the need never arises for advanced care.

Often, we can address long-term care needs with other solutions. One is life insurance containing long-term care provisions. And while these features are not a substitute for traditional long term care insurance, if a policyholder never needs to access those provisions, they can still use the cash

---

16 payingforseniorcare.com. 2022. "Long-Term Senior Care Statistics" https://www.payingforseniorcare.com/statistics

value component of their life insurance policy, or their beneficiaries can receive the death benefit.

In addition, some annuities contain income riders for long-term care. These can also be an appropriate way to help fund some long-term care expenses without requiring periodic price hikes to premiums.

A few relevant statistics to keep in mind:

- The longer you live, the more likely you are to continue living; the longer you live, the more health care you will likely need to pay for.
- The average cost of a private nursing home room in the United States is estimated to cost $9,872 a month in 2024.[17] But keep in mind, that is just the nursing home — it doesn't include other medical costs, let alone pleasantries, like entertainment or hobby spending.
- As referenced earlier, Fidelity calculated in a 2022 study that a healthy couple retiring at age sixty-five could expect to pay around $315,000 over the course of retirement to cover health and medical expenses.

I know. "Whoa, there, Bob, I was hoping to have a realistic idea of health costs, not be driven over by a cement mixer!"

The good news is, while we don't know these exact costs in advance, we know there *will* be costs. And you won't have to pay your total Medicare lifetime premiums in one day as a lump sum. Now that you have a good idea of health care costs in retirement, you can *plan* for them! That's the real point, here: Planning in advance can keep you from feeling nickel-and-dimed to your wits' end. Instead, having a sizeable portion of your assets earmarked for health care can allow you the freedom to choose health care networks, coverage options, and long-term care possibilities you like and that you think offer you the best in life.

---

[17] Jeff Hoyt. seniorliving.org. January 2, 2024. "How Much Does a Nursing Home Cost?" https://www.seniorliving.org/nursing-homes/costs/

Product Riders

LTCI and self-funding are not the only ways to plan for the expenses of longevity. Some companies are getting creative with their products, particularly insurance companies. One way they are retooling to meet people's needs is through optional product riders on annuities and life insurance. Elsewhere in this book, I talk about annuity basics, but here's a brief overview: Annuities are insurance contracts. You pay the insurance company a premium, either as a lump sum or as a series of payments over a set amount of time, in exchange for guaranteed income payments. One of the advantages of an annuity is it has access to riders, which allow you to tweak your contract for a fee, usually about 1 percent of the contract value annually. One annuity rider some companies offer is a long-term care rider. If you have an annuity with a long-term care rider and are not in need of long-term care, your contract behaves as any annuity contract would—nothing changes. Generally speaking, if you reach a point when you can't perform multiple functions of daily life on your own, you notify the insurance company, and a representative will turn on those provisions of your contract.

Like LTCI, different companies and products offer different options. Some annuity long-term care riders offer coverage of two years in a nursing home situation. Others cap expenses at two times the original annuity's value. It greatly depends. Some people prefer this option because there isn't a "use-it-or-lose-it" piece; if you die without ever having needed long-term care, you still will have had the income benefit from the base contract. Still, as with any annuities or insurance contracts, there are the usual restrictions and limitations. Withdrawing money from the contract will affect future income payments, early distributions can result in a penalty, income taxes may apply, and, because the insurance company's solvency is what guarantees your payments, it's important to do your research about the insurance company you are considering purchasing a contract from.

Understandably, a discussion on long-term care is bound to feel at least a little tedious. Yet, this is an important piece of planning for income in retirement, particularly if you want to leave a legacy.

Spousal Planning

Here's one thing to keep in mind no matter how you plan to save: Many of us will be planning for more than ourselves. Look back at all the stats on health events and the likelihood of long life and long-term care. If they hold true for a single individual, then the likelihood of having a costly health or long-term care event is even higher for a married couple. You'll be planning for not just one life, but two. So, when it comes to long-term care insurance, annuities, self-funding, or whatever strategy you are looking at using, be sure you are funding longevity for the both of you.

CHAPTER 2

Taxes

Where to begin with taxes? Perhaps by acknowledging we all bear responsibility for the resources we share. Roads, bridges, schools . . . it is the patriotic duty of every American to pay their fair share of taxes. Many would agree with me. However, while they don't mind paying their fair share, they're not interested in paying one cent more than that!

Now, just talking taxes probably takes your mind to April—tax season. You are probably thinking about all the forms you collect and how you file. Perhaps you are thinking about your certified public accountant or another qualified tax professional and saying to yourself, "I've already got taxes taken care of, thanks!"

However, what I see when people come into my office is that their relationship with their tax professional is purely a January through April relationship. That means they may have a tax professional, but not a tax *planner*.

What I mean is tax planning extends beyond filing taxes. In April, we are required to settle our accounts with the IRS to make sure we have paid up on our bill or to even the score if we have overpaid. But real tax planning is about making each financial move in a way that allows you to keep the most money in your pocket and out of Uncle Sam's.

Now, as a caveat, I want to emphasize I am neither a CPA nor a tax planner, but I see the way taxes affect my clients, and I have plenty of experience helping clients implement tax-efficient strategies in their retirement plans in conjunction with their tax professionals.

Most CPAs and accountants do fine work and a great job of mitigating potential tax problems by attempting to reduce your overall tax exposure from the previous year. They're often looking backward. I describe it as "looking through the rearview mirror." However, if you have tax-deferred accounts (IRAs, most 401(k)s, 403(b)s, SEPs, etc.), you know at some point there will be taxed required minimum distributions (RMDs) you must take from them. You also know the taxes on these distributions will have to be paid at that time. The problem is tax laws are regularly changing, and we really don't know what they will look like in the future. However, most agree that taxes likely will not decrease much in the future. So, the planning we do "looks through the windshield" and attempts to address potential problems before they become worse.

It is especially important to me to help my clients develop tax-efficient strategies in their retirement plans because each dollar they can keep is a dollar we can put to work.

We present many seminars around our community at local libraries and universities. The subjects we cover include Social Security, estate planning, investing for beginners, and more, but our most-attended events are always the tax presentations. People are very interested in reducing their tax exposure. Nearly everyone I speak to is perfectly fine paying their "fair share," but no one wants to pay more than that. The problem is that I believe there is a lack of quality information to help folks navigate tax traps, and the information available is often very confusing.

At these tax seminars, I always open with a simple question: "Do you think taxes are an important issue to retirement?" Nearly everyone in the room raises their hand "yes." I'm amazed at the reactions when I follow up with, "Now keep your hand raised if your financial advisor has asked to see your tax return within the last year." Often, an entire room of raised hands shrinks to just two or three. For those few, I'll finish my point by asking, "What did they do with the tax return? What type of tax strategies are they implementing?" These folks usually answer those questions with a deer in the headlights look—a blank stare. So, nearly everyone in the room believes tax planning is crucial to a quality retirement (they decided to spend ninety minutes with me at a tax class, after all), but many in these seminars are not getting any real tax-related assistance from their financial advisors. This is a real problem.

The Fed

Now, in the United States, taxes can be a rather uncertain proposition. Depending on who is in the White House and which party controls Congress, we might be tempted to assume tax rates could either decline or increase in the next four to eight years accordingly. However, there is one (large!) factor we, as a nation, must confront: the national debt.

Currently, according to USDebtClock.org, we are over $34,000,000,000,000 in debt and climbing. That's $34 *trillion* with a "T." With just $1 trillion, you could park it in the bank at a zero percent interest rate and spend more than $54 million every day for fifty years without hitting a zero balance.

Even if Congress got a handle and stopped that debt from its daily compound, divided by each taxpayer, we each would owe about $264,000. So, will that be check, cash, or Venmo?[18]

My point here isn't to give you anxiety. I'm just cautioning you that even with the rosiest of outlooks on our personal income tax rates, none of us should count on low tax rates for the long term. Instead, you and your network of professionals (tax, legal, and financial) should constantly be looking for ways to take advantage of tax-saving opportunities as they come. After all, the best "luck" is when proper planning meets opportunity.

So, how can we get started?

---

[18] usdebtclock.org. Accessed January 22, 2024.

Know Your Limits

One of the foundational pieces of tax planning is knowing what tax bracket you are in, based on your income after subtracting pre-tax or untaxed assets. Your income taxes are based on your taxable income.

One reason to know your taxable income and your income tax rate is so you can see how far away you are from the next lower or higher tax bracket. This is particularly important when it comes to decisions such as gifting and Roth IRA rollovers.

Assuming a Lower Tax Rate

Many people anticipate being in a lower tax bracket in retirement. It makes sense: You won't be contributing to retirement funds; you'll be drawing from them. And you won't have all those work expenses—work clothes, transportation, lunch meetings, etc.

Yet, do you really plan on changing your lifestyle after retirement? Do you plan to cut down on the number of times you eat out, scale back vacations, and skimp on travel?

What I see in my office is many couples spend more in the first few years, or maybe the first decade, of retirement. Sure, that may taper off later on, but usually only just in time for their budget to be hit with greater health and long-term care expenses. Do you see where this is going? Many people plan as though their taxable income will be lower in retirement and are surprised when the tax bills come in and look more or less the same as they used to. It's better to plan for the worst and hope for the best, wouldn't you agree?

401(k)/IRA

One sometimes-unexpected piece of tax planning in retirement concerns your 401(k) or IRA. Most of us have one of these accounts or an equivalent. Throughout our working lives, we pay in, dutifully socking away a portion of our earnings in these tax-deferred accounts. There's the rub: tax-deferred. Not tax-free. Very rarely is anything free of taxation when you get down to it. Using 401(k)s and IRAs in retirement is no different. The taxes the government deferred when you were in your working years are now coming due, and you will pay taxes on that income at whatever your current tax rate is.

Just to ensure Uncle Sam gets his due, the government also has a required minimum distribution, or RMD, rule. Beginning at age seventy-three, you are required to withdraw a certain minimum amount every year from your 401(k) or IRA, or else you will face a tax penalty on any RMD monies you should have withdrawn but didn't—and that's on top of income tax. The SECURE Act 2.0 reduced the penalty to 25 percent (from 50 percent). Timely corrections also can reduce the penalty to 10 percent.[19]

Of course, there is also the Roth account. You can think of the difference between a Roth and a traditional retirement account as the difference between taxing the seed and taxing the harvest. Because Roths are funded with post-tax dollars, there aren't tax penalties for early withdrawals of the principal nor are there taxes on the growth after you reach age fifty-nine-and-one-half. Perhaps best of all, there are no RMDs. Of course, you must own a Roth account for a minimum of five years before you are able to take advantage of all its features.

This is one more area where it pays to be aware of your tax bracket. Some people may find it advantageous to "convert" their traditional retirement account funds to Roth account funds in a year during which they are in a lower tax bracket. Others may opt to put any excess RMDs from their traditional retirement accounts into other products, like stocks or insurance.

Does that make your head spin? Understandable. That's why it's so important to work with a financial professional and tax

---

[19] Jim Probasco. Investopedia.com. January 6, 2023. "SECURE 2.0 Act of 2022." https://www.investopedia.com/secure-2-0-definition-5225115

planner who can help you execute these sorts of tax-efficient strategies and help you understand what you are doing and why.

As important as tax strategies are, we can't forget their place in an overall retirement plan. It has been my experience that for most, investment strategies are usually prioritized over tax planning, which comes in at a close second. I often tell people, "We don't let the tax tail wag the investment dog."

CHAPTER 3

Market Volatility

U p and down. Roller coaster. Merry-go-round. Bulls and bears. Peak-to-trough.

Sound familiar? This is the language we use to talk about the stock market. With volatility and spikes, even our language is jarring, bracing, and vivid.

Still, financial strategies tend to revolve around market-based products, for good reasons. For one thing, there is no other financial class that packs the same potential for growth, pound for pound, as stock-based products. Because of growth potential, inflation challenges, and new opportunities, it may be unwise to avoid the market entirely.

However, along with the potential for growth is the potential for loss. At the time this book was written, many of the people I've seen in my office came in feeling uneasy because of the economic fallout of the COVID-19 outbreak of 2020, followed by the economic downturn, and the inflation spike that happened in 2022.

So how do we balance these factors? How do we try to satisfy both the need for protection and the need for growth?

For one thing, it is important to recognize the value of diversity. Now, I'm not just talking about the diversity of assets among different kinds of stocks, or even different kinds of stocks and bonds. That's only one kind of diversity; while important, both stocks and bonds, though different, are both still market-based products. Most market-based products, even within a diverse portfolio, tend to rise or lower as a whole, just like an incoming tide. Therefore, a portfolio diverse in only market-sourced products won't automatically preserve your assets during times when the market declines.

In addition to the sort of "horizontal diversity" you have by purchasing a variety of stocks and bonds from different companies, I also suggest you think about "vertical diversity," or diversity among asset classes. This means having different product types, including securities products, bank products, and insurance products—with varying levels of growth potential, liquidity, and protection—all in accordance with your unique situation, goals, and needs.

I look at risk tolerance like measuring a room in your house to build a second floor. What would you guess the distance is from the wall on your left to the wall on your right? I'm sure your "guesstimate" is pretty close, but would that "guesstimate" be a sufficient measurement to give to a general contractor? Most would agree it's best to actually measure it with a measuring tape. Once you do this, you may find you are off by many inches and sometimes many feet. That could easily result in a deviation of 20 percent or more! The difference is measuring based on a gut feeling or emotion rather than on an actual measurement. When gauging your risk tolerance, it's important to have a quantifiable measurement to inform your decisions, not just a guess.

From my experience, when addressing risk tolerance, most financial advisors begin by asking what you would do if the market went down by 30 percent. Would you buy more because the market is at a discount? Get out because you're scared you may lose more? Or just do nothing? Conversely, what would you do if the market was up 30 percent? Buy more because the market is good? Get out because the market may be at a peak? Or, again, do nothing?

The advisor then tells you, based on their analysis, that you are "moderately conservative." You may ask, "What exactly does moderately conservative mean?"

And the advisor may reply, "Don't worry about that. We will match you up perfectly with a moderately conservative portfolio." The problem with this approach is that it's akin to just guessing the distance in the room. This guess is probably pretty close but could also end up being off by 20 percent or more!

We take a much more quantitative approach and actually measure your risk tolerance by giving it a "risk score" from one to 100. We accomplish this with an industry software program The higher the risk score, the more risk tolerance you may have. This is all predicated around one simple question: How much of your investment are you willing to risk in a six-month period? I ask folks to tell me the number and not a percentage because I feel like losses (and gains) can sometimes be camouflaged in a percentage point. Actual dollars lost usually feel different. We follow that up with a few more questions based on the dollar amounts of a risk versus reward scenario. The final output of this scenario is a quantifiable risk score between one and 100.

Think of the speed you're willing to drive to get to a destination. If you drive really fast, you may get to your destination faster, but you may also be more likely to wreck your car. On the other hand, if you're willing to drive slower, it will probably take you longer to reach your destination, but you may be less likely to be in an accident.

The Color of Money

When you're looking at the overall diversity of your portfolio, part of the equation is knowing which products fit in what category: what has liquidity, what has protection, and what has growth potential.

Before we dive in, keep in mind these aren't absolutes. You might think of liquidity, growth, and protection as primary colors. While some products will look pretty much yellow, red, or blue, others will have a mix of characteristics, making them more green, orange, or purple.

Growth

I like to think of the growth category as red. It's powerful, it's somewhat volatile, and it's also the category where we have the greatest opportunities for growth and loss. Often, products in the growth category will have a good deal of liquidity but very little protection. These are our market-based products and strategies, and we think of them mostly in shades of red and orange, to designate their growth and liquidity. This is a good place to be when you're young—think fast cars and flashy leather jackets—but its allure often wanes as you move closer to retirement. Examples of "red" products include:

- Stocks
- Equities
- Exchange-traded funds
- Mutual funds
- Corporate bonds
- Real estate investment trusts
- Speculations
- Alternative investments

Liquidity

Yellow is my liquid category color. I typically recommend having at least enough yellow money to cover six months' to a year's worth of expenses in case of emergency. Yellow assets don't need a lot of growth potential; they just need to be readily available when we need them. The "yellow" category includes assets like:

- Cash
- Money market accounts

Protection

The color of protection, to me, is blue, which can incorporate products such as annuities. Tranquil, peaceful, sure, even if it lacks a certain amount of flash. This is the direction I like to see people generally move toward as they're nearing retirement. The red, flashy look of stock market returns and the risk of possible overnight losses is less attractive as we near retirement and look for more consistency and reliability. While this category doesn't come with a lot of liquidity, the products here are backed by an insurance company, a bank, or a government entity. "Blue" products include things such as:

- Certificates of deposit (backed by banks)
- Government-based bonds (backed by the U.S. government)
- Life insurance (backed by insurance companies)
- Annuities (backed by insurance companies)

When investing money with a market-based philosophy, we usually use a "core/satellite" approach. The "core" model is usually a very broad, well-diversified, and passively managed model based on your specific risk score. It may be as much as 50 percent or more of your entire portfolio. We then surround that core model with a handful of "satellite" models that are usually managed differently.

For an after-tax account, we would look to use a tax-efficient model. For a Roth IRA, we may use a model that is in a slightly higher risk score than you're comfortable with, but we can balance that with another satellite model that has no correlation to the stock market and has a lower risk score.

We look not only at your risk score with these satellite models but the underlying investments, management philosophy (passive versus tactical versus strategic, etc.), tax efficiency, and more. This core/satellite philosophy is great for diversification but also adds an element of purpose to what we're doing.

401(k)s

I want to take a second to specifically address a product many retirees will be using to build their retirement income: the 401(k) and other retirement accounts. Any of these retirement accounts (IRAs, 401(k)s, 403(b)s, etc.) are basically "tax wrappers." What do I mean by that? Well, depending on your plan provider, a 401(k) could include target-date funds, passively managed products, stocks, bonds, mutual funds, or even variable, fixed, and fixed index annuities, all collected in one place and governed by rules (a.k.a. the "tax wrapper"). These rules govern how much money you can put inside, what ways you can put it in, when you will pay taxes on it, and when you can take the money out. Inside the 401(k), each of the products inside the "tax wrapper" might have its own fees or commissions, in addition to the management fee you pay on the 401(k) itself.

Now, fees can be troublesome. You can't get something for nothing, and fees are how many financial companies and professionals make a living. Yet, it's important to recognize even a fee with a fraction of a percentage point is money out of your pocket—money that represents not just the one-time fee of today but also represents an opportunity cost. A $100,000 IRA that earns 6 percent over a twenty-five-year period without investment fees would earn $430,000. But if just a 0.5 percent fee got factored into that investment, the IRA would be worth $379,000 in twenty-five years, a $50,500 decrease.[20] For someone close to retirement, how much do you think fees may have cost over their lifetime?

Even for those close to retirement, it's important to look at management fees and assess if you think you're getting what you pay for. Over the course of ten years, those costs can add

---

[20] Pam Krueger. Kiplinger.com. January 8, 2021. "How to Spot (and Squash) Nasty Fees That Hide in Your Investments" https://www.kiplinger.com/retirement/retirement-planning/602043/how-to-spot-and-squash-nasty-fees-that-hide-in-your

up, and you may have decades ahead of you in which you will need to rely on your assets.

Dollar-Cost Averaging

With 401(k)s and other market-based retirement products, dollar-cost averaging is a concept that can work in your favor when you are investing for the long term. When the market is trending up, if you are consistently paying in money, month over month, great; your investments can grow, and you are adding to your assets. When the market takes a dip, no problem; your dollars buy more shares at a lower price. At some point, we hope the market will rebound, in which case your shares can grow and possibly be more valuable than they were before. This concept is what we call "dollar-cost averaging." While it can't ensure a profit or guarantee against losses, it's a time-tested strategy for investing in a volatile market.

However, when you are in retirement, this strategy may work against you. You may have heard of "reverse" dollar-cost averaging. Before, when the market lost ground, you were "bargain-shopping"; your dollars purchased more assets at a reduced price. When you are in retirement, you are no longer the purchaser; you are selling. So, in a down market, you have to sell more assets to make the same amount of money as what you made in a favorable market.

I've had lots of people step into my office to talk to me about this, emphasizing, "my advisor says the market always bounces back, and I have to just hold on for the long term."

There's some basis for this thinking; thus far, the market has always rebounded to higher heights than before. But this is no guarantee, and the prospect of potentially higher returns in five years may not be very helpful in retirement if you are relying on the income from those returns to pay this month's electric bill, for example.

There's a difference between working with an independent financial professional and a captive one. An independent professional isn't usually tied to one company or philosophy. They have many options to choose from. However, a captive professional usually works for a large investment firm or insurance company. Regardless of the issue or concern you may have, their answer is usually going to be a recommendation from that company.

Independent professionals usually have different companies (sometimes many) they can work with, but they typically have other options as well. As an independent advisor, I compare investment- and insurance-based products to tools you would use. Let's think of these tools like gardening. Each tool has a purpose and does its job really well, but each also does the others' jobs poorly.

If you were raking leaves in your yard, what tool would you use? A rake, of course. But what if I came along and suggested you should use a shovel to rake the leaves? What would you say to me? "That's crazy! A shovel doesn't rake leaves very well." A rake is a perfect tool for that job. After a good laugh, what if I said, "Ok, let's take that rake and try to dig a hole or chop down a shrub." Again, you would probably accuse me of being crazy because a rake would be unable to accomplish either of those tasks—at least, not very well. Tools have purposes. There are "salespeople" in the financial industry who might, for example, try to convince you that a shovel is the best tool to rake leaves or that a rake is the best tool to chop a shrub down simply because these are the only tools they have to "sell" you. Working with an independent professional instead of a captive one can usually help with this issue.

Is There a "Perfect" Product?

To bring us back around to the discussion of protection, growth, and liquidity, the ideal product would be a "ten" in all three categories, right? Completely guaranteed, doubling in size every few years, and accessible whenever you want. Does such a product exist? Absolutely not.

Instead of running in circles looking for that perfect product, the silver bullet, the unicorn of financial strategies, it's more important to circle back to the concept of a balanced, asset-diverse portfolio.

This is why your goals may be better served when you work with a knowledgeable financial professional who knows what various financial products can do and how to use them in your personal retirement strategy.[*]

---

[*] Investing involves risk, including the potential loss of principal. No investment strategy can guarantee a profit or protect against loss in periods of declining values. Any references to protection benefits or guaranteed/lifetime income streams refer only to fixed insurance products, not securities or investment products. Insurance and annuity product guarantees are backed by the financial strength and claims-paying ability of the issuing insurance company.

Insurance products are offered through the insurance business Nu Venture Financial Group. Nu Venture Financial Group is also an Investment Advisory practice that offers products and services through AE Wealth Management, LLC (AEWM), a Registered Investment Advisor. AEWM does not offer insurance products. The insurance products offered by Nu Venture Financial Group are not subject to investment Advisor requirements.

CHAPTER 4

Retirement Income

etirement. For many of us, it's what we've saved for and dreamed of, pinning our hopes to a magical someday. Is that someday full of traveling? Is it filled with grandkids? Gardening? Maybe your fondest dream is simply never having to work again, never having to clock in or be accountable to someone else.

Your ability to do these things all hinges on *income*. Without the money to support these dreams, even a basic level of work-free lifestyle is unsustainable. That's why planning for your income in retirement is so foundational. But where do we begin?

It's easy to feel overwhelmed by this question. Some may feel the urge to amass a large lump sum and then try to put it all in one product—insurance, investments, liquid assets—to provide all the growth, liquidity, and income they need. Instead, I think you need a more balanced approach. After all, retirement planning isn't magic. As I mention elsewhere, there is no single product that can be all things to all people (or even all things to one person). No approach works unilaterally for everyone. That's why it's important to talk to a financial professional who can help you lay down the basics and take you step-by-step through the process. Not only will you have the assurance to address the areas you need, but you will also have an ally who can help you break down the process and help keep you from feeling overwhelmed.

Sources of Income

Thinking of all the pieces of your retirement expenses might be intimidating. But, like cleaning out a junk drawer or revisiting that garage remodel, once you have laid everything out, you can begin to sort things into categories.

Once you have a good overall picture of where your expenses will lie, you can start stacking up the resources to cover them.

Social Security

Social Security is a guaranteed, inflation-protected federal insurance program that plays a significant part in most of our retirement plans. From delaying until you've reached full retirement age or beyond to examining spousal benefits, as I discuss elsewhere in this book, there is plenty you can do to try to make the most of this monthly benefit. As with all your retirement income sources, it's important to consider how to make this resource stretch to provide the most bang and buck for your situation.

Pension

Another generally reliable source of retirement income for you might be a pension, if you are one of the lucky people who still has one.

If you don't have a pension, go ahead and skim on to the next section. If you do have a pension, keep on reading.

Because your pension can be such a central piece of your retirement income plan, you will want to put some thought into answering basic questions about it.

How well is your pension funded? Since the heyday of the pension plan, companies and governments have neglected to fund their pension obligations, causing a persistent problem with this otherwise reliable asset.

Consider the factors at play, though. Pensions had been underfunded and gained a boost from strong market performance in 2021. What happens to the solvency of those pension funds if the market declines?

It can be worthwhile to keep tabs on your pension's health and know what your options are for withdrawing your pension. If you have already retired and made those decisions, this may be a foregone conclusion. If not, it pays to know what you can expect and what decisions you can make, such as taking spousal options to cover your husband or wife if he or she outlives you.

Also, some companies are incentivizing lump-sum payouts of pensions to reduce the companies' payment liabilities. If that's the case with your employer, talk to your financial professional to see if it might be prudent to do something like that or if it might be better to stick with lifetime payments or other options.

Your 401(k) and IRA

One "modern way" to save for retirement is in a 401(k) or IRA (or their nonprofit or governmental equivalents). These tax-advantaged accounts are, in my opinion, a poor substitute for pensions, but one of the biggest disservices we do to ourselves is to not take full advantage of them in the first place. According to one article, only 41 percent of Americans invest in a 401(k), though 68 percent of employed Americans have access to a 401(k) benefit option.[21]

Also, if you have changed jobs over the years, do the work of tracking down any benefits from your past employers. You might have an IRA here or a 401(k) there; keep track of those so you can pull them together and look at those assets when you're ready to look at establishing sources of retirement income.

---

[21] Amin Dabit. personalcapital.com. April 1, 2021. "The Average 401k Balance by Age." https://www.personalcapital.com/blog/retirement-planning/average-401k-balance-age/

Do You Have...

- Life insurance?
- Annuities?
- Long-term care insurance?
- Any passive income sources?
- Stock and bond portfolios?
- Liquid assets? (What's in your bank account?)
- Alternative investments?
- Rental properties?

If you are going through the work of sitting with a financial professional, it's important to look at your full retirement income picture and pull together *all* your assets, no matter how big or small. From the free insurance policy offered at your bank to the sizable investment in your brother-in-law's modestly successful furniture store, you want to have a good idea of where your money is.

Many families come into my office with huge lingering questions on their minds: Do I have enough? Can I retire? And if I can, what does my retirement look like? They usually know approximately how much they've saved and have a rough idea of their budget, but they often aren't equipped to put all the pieces together to craft a retirement income plan that can navigate the many risks and pitfalls one may encounter in retirement: stock market volatility, inflation, taxes, healthcare expenses, Social Security, and more.

My goal in retirement planning is to give each family I work with the confidence to retire. This usually comes in one of three ways:

1. You can fully retire now, and this is how it will look.
2. You can retire now but with some conditions. You may have to work part-time for a while to bridge the income gap and fortify your future retirement income stream.
3. You can retire at a certain date in the future after you achieve certain goals. This may include saving more for a few more years, continuing to work full-time for a few

more years, avoiding taking a huge loss due to a market downturn, or paying down some debt.

This is the point that gives me, as a professional, more enjoyment than anything else I do: when you tell and show someone ways they can retire, and you watch their face light up and their anxiety fade away. For me, this is what it's all about; it's why I do what I do.

Retirement Income Needs

How much income will you need in retirement? How do you determine that? A lot of people work toward a random number, thinking, "If I can just have a million dollars, I'll be comfortable in retirement!" Don't get me wrong; it is possible to save up a lot of money and then retire in the hopes you can keep your monthly expenses lower than some set estimation. But I think this carries a general risk of running out of money. Instead, I work with my clients to find out what their current and projected income needs are and then work from there to see how we might cover any gaps between what they have and what they want.

Goals and Dreams

I like to start with your pie in the sky. Do you find yourself planning for your vacations more thoroughly than you do your retirement? Maybe it's because planning a vacation is less stressful: Having a week at the beach go awry is, well, a walk on the beach compared to running out of money in retirement. Whatever the case, perhaps it would be better if you thought of your retirement as a vacation in and of itself—no clocking in, no boss, no overtime. If you felt unlimited by financial strain, what would you do?

Would an endless vacation for you mean Paris and Rome? Would it mean mentoring at children's clubs or serving at the local soup kitchen? Or maybe it would mean deepening your ties to those immediately around you—neighbors, friends, and family. Maybe it would mean more time to take part in the hobbies and activities you love. Have you been considering a second (or even third) act as a small-business owner, turning a hobby or passion into a revenue source?

This is your time to daydream and answer the question: If you could do anything, what would you do?

After that, it's a matter of putting a dollar amount on it. What are the costs of round-the-world travel? One couple I know said their highest priority in retirement was being able to take each of their grandchildren on a cross-country vacation every year. That's a pretty specific goal—one that is reasonably easy to nail down a budget for.

When someone comes into our office for a first visit, we ask them to bring their written income plan for analysis. Many times, they don't even have a written income plan, but if they do, they usually bring a "Monte Carlo" analysis. Those are simulations used to help explain the impact of risk and uncertainty in prediction and forecasting models.

This income analyzer will evaluate your income, expenses, and investments. It will also run your scenario through up to 1,000 different stock market iterations to predict a probability of success score. Just for fun, let's say someone's analytical score is 90 percent. Sounds pretty good, right? And the consumer may feel as if their retirement future is reasonably secure.

But think about it. A 90 percent chance of reaching a destination on an airplane would lead most people to flee from the airport. A 90 percent chance of your new home's foundation holding up would also seem substandard. Such odds would be inappropriate to us when using a fiscal house approach in which your income plan serves as the foundation of your retirement plan. While these examples may seem extreme, they do serve to illustrate how risk is relative. For some things, like test scores or an event turnout, 90 percent is a fantastic number. For other things, even that high a number can still be insufficient.

So then, is a 90 percent score based on "Monte Carlo" income analysis truly satisfactory? This is your retirement. You don't want to take on even the slightest chance of running out of money.

NuVenture Financial Group does not use "Monte Carlo" simulations to build retirement income plans. We build plans based on combining all income streams someone can draw from in retirement and accounting for different variables that can arise. And while no one can 100 percent guarantee a retirement plan, our process is thorough. We're not looking for a percentage (such as 90 percent) we deem acceptable, but rather a plan clients can rely on and modify if necessary that lasts for the duration of their retirement.

Current Budget

In my experience, compiling a current expense report is one of the trickiest pieces of retirement preparation. Many people assume the expenses of their lives in retirement will be different—lower. After all, there will be no drive to work, no need for a formal wardrobe, and, perhaps most impactful of all, no more saving for retirement!

Yet, we often underestimate our daily spending habits. That's why I typically ask my clients to bring in their bank statements for the past year—they are reflective of your *actual* spending, not just what you think you're spending.

One of the very first bits of information we try to get from a new prospective client at (or before) their first visit with us is their monthly expenses. Most folks will just do a quick rudimentary tally of what they think their expenses are, and others will complete a budget worksheet or already have a spreadsheet prepared. Here's the problem: those ways of estimating expenses are often wrong. Sometimes they are off by 15 to 20 percent or more per month. If I'm going to help you craft a successful retirement plan, this monthly expense number is arguably the most important number we need to begin with, so we have to get it right the first time.

The way we arrive at your monthly expenses is surprisingly easy, quick, and accurate. Most everyone reading this has online banking and can easily look at their bank statements. We ask that you look at your twelve most recent bank statements (no need to print or download them—just view them) and extract just one number from each statement: the sum of your total withdrawals, or debits. It's usually one number at the top or bottom of your statement. Take that number from each of the last twelve months, add them together, and divide that number by twelve. This formula will give your average monthly expenses in most normal cases. However, there are some cases where this doesn't work quite so well, so it's taken on a case-by-case basis.

As you're doing this exercise, you may notice some abnormally high months during the year. These high months may be where you had some anomaly like a large vacation, home improvement, or another large expense. We ask that you extract those items from the total because they're one-time expenses, not monthly. We account and budget for those one-time expenses separately, but for this exercise, we're just looking for average expenses. The beauty of this exercise is that no expenses are hidden. Usually, every bill you pay will eventually show up on your bank statement at some point.

I can't count the number of times I have sat with a couple, asked them about their spending, and heard them throw out a number that seemed incredibly low. When I ask them where the number came from, they usually say they estimated based on their total bills. Yet, our spending is so much more than our mortgage, utilities, cable, phone, car, grocery, or credit card bills.

"What about clothes?" I ask, "Or dining out? What about gifts and coffees and last-minute birthday cards?" That's when the lights come on.

This is why I suggest collecting a year's worth of information. There is usually no such thing as a one-time purchase. Did you buy new furniture? Even if that is a rarity, do you think that will be the last time you *ever* buy furniture?

Often, when you ask someone about their monthly budget, they'll quickly blurt out an estimate without thinking too much about their spending habits. Others may actually keep a spreadsheet of expenses, but some fall into the category of not keeping up with logging purchases or bills into the spreadsheet.

So again, I want to emphasize the straightforward method we advocate for calculating a budget. It takes very little time. To repeat, go into your bank account and pull the previous twelve statements indicative of a year's worth of expenditures. There's no need even to print them out. Instead, add the totals for each month.

Then, review each month's statement to determine any outliers—an anomaly that surfaces (a new roof, hearing aids, or a vacation cruise are examples) Such expenses can be removed from the budgeting exercise but must be accounted through different aspects used in developing a viable retirement income plan.

Once all the regular expenses for a twelve-month period are accounted for and averaged per month, it can be an eye-opening experience for many. They typically realize they spend more per month than they estimated. And, the expenses listed will account for inflationary increases because the overview reflects real-time costs. I feel this relatively simple exercise is better and often more accurate than having people fill out budget worksheets.

Another hefty expense is spending on the kids. Many of the couples I work with are quick to help their adult children, whether it's something like letting them live in the basement, paying for college, babysitting, paying an occasional bill, or contributing to a grandchild's college fund. Research concluded that 22 percent of adults receive some kind of financial support from parents. That segment jumps to almost 30 percent when factoring the generation we call millennials.[22]

---

[22] Kamaron McNair. magnifymoney.com. October 26, 2021. "Nearly 30% of Millennials Still Receive Financial Support From Their Parents" https://www.magnifymoney.com/blog/news/parental-financial-support-survey/

My clients sometimes protest that what they do for their grown children can stop in retirement. They don't *need* to help. But I get it. Parents like to feel needed. And, while you never want to neglect saving for retirement in favor of taking on financial risks (like your child's student debt), the parents who help their adult children do so in part because it helps them feel fulfilled.

When it comes down to expenses, including (and especially) spending on your family, don't make your initial calculations based on what you *could* whittle your budget down to if you *had* to. Instead, start from where you are. Who wants to live off a bare-bones bank account in retirement?

Other Expenses

Once you have nailed down your current budget and your dreams or goals for retirement, there are a few other outstanding pieces to think about—some expenses many people don't take the time to consider before making and executing a plan. But I'm assuming you want to get it right, so let's take a look.

Housing

Do you know where you want to live in retirement? This makes up a substantial piece of your income puzzle—since the typical American household owns a home, and it's generally their largest asset.

Some people prefer to live right where they are for as long as they can. Others have been waiting for retirement to pull the trigger on an ambitious move, like purchasing a new house, or even downsizing. Whatever your plans and whatever your reasons, there are quite a few things to consider.

Mortgage

Do you still have a mortgage? What may have been a nice tax boon in your working years could turn into a financial burden in your retirement. After all, when you are on a limited income, a mortgage is just one more bill sapping your financial strength. It is something to put some thought into, whether you plan to age in place or are considering moving to your dream home, buying a house out of state, or living in a retirement community.

Upkeep and Taxes

A house without a mortgage still requires annual taxes. While it's tempting to think of this as a once-a-year expense, when you have limited earning potential, your annual tax bill might be something into which you should put a little more forethought.

The costs of homeownership aren't just monetary. When you find yourself dealing with more house than you need, it can drain your time and energy. From keeping clutter at bay to keeping the lawn mower running, upkeep can be extensive and expensive. For some, that's a challenge they heartily accept and can comfortably take on. For others, the idea of yard work or cleaning an area larger than they need feels foolish.

For instance, Peggy discovered after her knee replacement that most of her house was inaccessible to her when she was laid up.

"It felt ridiculous to pay someone else to dust and vacuum a house I was only living in 40 percent of!"

Practicality and Adaptability

Erik and Magda are looking to retire within the next two decades. They just sold their old three-bedroom ranch-style house. Their twins are in high school, and the couple has wanted to "upgrade" for years. Now they live in a gorgeous 1940s three-story house with all the kitchen space they ever wanted, five sprawling bedrooms, and a library and media room for themselves and their children. Within months of moving in, the couple realized a house perfect for their active teens would no longer be perfect for them in five to fifteen years.

"We are paying the mortgage for this house, but we've started saving for the next one," said Magda, "because who wants to climb two flights of stairs to their bedroom when they're seventy-eight?"

Others I know have encountered a similar situation in their personal lives. After a health crisis, one couple found the luxurious tub for two they toiled to install had become a specter of a bad slip and a potential safety risk. It's important to think through what your physical reality could be. I always emphasize to my clients that they should plan for whatever their long-term future might hold, but it's amazing how many people don't give it much thought.

Contracts and Regulations

If you are looking into a cross-country move, be aware of new tax tables or local ordinances in the area where you are looking to move. After all, you don't want to experience sticker-shock when you are looking at downsizing or reducing your bills in retirement.

Along the same lines, if you are moving into a retirement community, be sure to look at the fine print. What happens if you must move into a different situation for long-term care? Will you be penalized? Will you be responsible for replacing your slot in the community? What are all the fees, and what do they cover?

Inflation

As I write this in 2024, America has experienced a wave of inflation following a lengthy period of low inflation. Inflation zoomed to 9.1 percent in June 2022, its highest mark since

November 1981.[23] In 2023, the inflation rate decreased to 3.1 percent.[24]

Core inflation is yet another measurement that excludes goods with prices that tend to be more volatile, such as food and energy costs. Core inflation for a twelve-month period ending in December 2022 was 5.7 percent. It so happened that energy prices rose 7.3 percent over that timeframe.[25]

However, inflation isn't a one-time bump; it has a cumulative effect. Again, that can impact the price of groceries more than other goods. Even with relatively low inflation over the past few decades, an item you bought in 1997 for $2 will cost about $3.70 today.[26] Want to go to a show? A $20 ticket in 1997 would cost $43.01 in 2023.[27]

As you can see in the following chart, the prices of items you've purchased in the past ten years could have been wildly different depending on when you bought them.

What if we hit a stretch in retirement like the late seventies and early eighties, when annual inflation rates of 10 percent became the norm? It may be wise to consider some extra padding in your retirement income plan to account for any potential increase in inflation in the future.

---

[23] tradingeconomics.com. 2022 Data/2023 Forecast/1914-2021 Historical. "United States Inflation Rate" https://tradingeconomics.com/united-states/inflation-cpi

[24] statistica.com. December 13, 2023. "Monthly 12-month inflation rate in the United States from November 2020 to November 2023" https://www.statista.com/statistics/273418/unadjusted-monthly-inflation-rate-in-the-us

[25] U.S. Inflation Calculator. "United States Core Inflation Rates (1957-2022)" https://www.usinflationcalculator.com/inflation/united-states-core-inflation-rates/

[26] In2013dollars.com. "$2 in 1997 is worth $3.70 today" https://www.in2013dollars.com/us/inflation/1997?amount=2

[27] In2013dollars.com "Admission to movies, theaters, and concerts priced at $20 in 1997>$40.34 in 2022" https://www.in2013dollars.com/Admission-to-movies,-theaters,-and-concerts/price-inflation

Aging

Also, in the expense category, think about longevity. We all hope to age gracefully. However, it's important to face the prospect of aging with a sense of realism.

The elephant in the room for many families is long-term care. No one wants to admit they will likely need it, but estimates indicate almost 70 percent of us will.[28] Aging is a significant piece of retirement income planning because you'll want to figure out how to set aside money for your care, either at home or away from it. The more comfortable you get with discussing your wishes and plans with your loved ones, the easier planning for the financial side of it can be.

I denote health care and potential long-term care costs in more detail elsewhere in this book, but suffice it to say nursing home care tends to be very expensive and typically isn't something you get to choose when you will need.

It isn't just the costs of long-term care that pose a concern in living longer. It's also about covering the possible costs of everything else associated with living longer. For instance, if Henry retires from his job as a biochemical engineer at age sixty-five, perhaps he planned to have a very decent income for twenty years, until age eighty-five. But what if he lives until he's ninety-five? That's a whole third—ten years—more of personal income he will need.

Putting It All Together

Whew! So, you have pulled together what you have, and you have a pretty good idea of where you want to be. Now your financial professional and you can go about the work of arranging what assets you *have* to cover what you *need*—and how you might try to cover any gaps.

---

[28] Moll Law Group. 2022. "The Cost of Long-Term Care." https://www.molllawgroup.com/the-cost-of-long-term-care.html

Like the proverbial man in the Bible who built his house on a rock, I like to help my clients figure out how to cover their day-to-day living expenses—their needs—with insurance and other guaranteed income sources like pensions and Social Security.

When I'm beginning to work with a new family to figure out their retirement plan, I usually review our "fiscal house" analogy used to describe building a sound retirement plan.

If we were going to build a house together, we would probably start with the foundation. Like your own home, we need to make sure this foundation is solid and has no cracks. The foundation of a retirement plan is a reliable monthly income stream. This income stream needs to equal or exceed your monthly expenses. Some sources of reliable income would be Social Security, a pension, or rent from an investment property. However, if this income is not enough to fulfill your monthly obligations, then we'll need to supplement it with additional income from your investments. There are a few ways to accomplish this additional income, but we aim to use only as much of your investments as necessary to fill that income gap and not a penny more. Once we've laid the foundation, our goal is to have built an income stream that will last a lifetime.

After the foundation is complete, it's time to build the walls. The "walls" are the money we allocate for the next ten to fifteen years in retirement. Most of the families I work with want to do similar things in their early retirement. We call these the "go-go" years—when you are spending and enjoying the money you've saved during your working years. Most folks tell me they want to travel, make some home improvements, help their family, or buy items like boats, RVs, and motorcycles.

These years are what you've been waiting for, and I encourage you to "spend the money" within reason. We all have one life to live—seize the day! We don't want to budget for these large expenses monthly because they usually don't occur monthly. We budget for them differently. The money we invest in the "walls" is often invested in a conservative stock market account for accessibility. These funds can usually be transferred into your checking account within two to three business days. So, when these obligations come up, we just transfer the appropriate amount of funds into your checking account.

Once the foundation is laid and the walls are up, we can work on the "roof." Money allocated to the roof is for expenses we think you will encounter fifteen years and beyond into your retirement—the "slow-go" years. We'll need to plan for potentially higher medical expenses to address possible assisted living or nursing home situations. We'll talk about legacy planning—how do you want to leave your estate once you've passed? Having a sound estate plan, life insurance, and charitable giving is addressed here. Lastly, we need to plan for inflation. In my experience, as long as the income foundation is well thought-out, inflation usually doesn't become much of an issue for ten years or more. Eventually, however, it must be addressed, so we'll need to plan for it to supplement your income at that point.

Now, the funds we allocate in the roof to address those specific concerns can have a little different "flavor." With these funds, we can choose to be a little more aggressive with our risk exposure in the stock market (if your personal risk tolerance allows for it) because we have a longer time horizon. We might also use vehicles that have a longer time commitment, like a fixed-indexed annuity, if it makes sense for your situation.

The last part of building the "fiscal house" is addressing emergency needs. If your home were to catch on fire, do you have a quick way of getting out? An emergency exit? More than likely, that is the case, and we're going to make sure we've planned for an appropriate amount of money to help you maintain an "emergency exit" in your fiscal house—a good, old-fashioned savings account at your bank or credit union. These funds aren't managed by us, but during regular reviews with our clients, we make sure we ask about their savings accounts. This is money that should be able to be withdrawn within the same day to address immediate concerns.

Once we've allocated all funds appropriately and your fiscal house is built, we always remind our clients things may change in the future due to unforeseen events. The fiscal house we build will be flexible and can evolve over the years as the lives of our clients evolve.

Again, you should keep in mind there isn't one single financial vehicle, asset, or source to fill all your needs, and that's okay. One of the challenges of planning for your income in retirement concerns figuring out what products and strategies to use. You can release some of that stress when you accept the fact you will probably need a diverse portfolio—potentially with bonds, stocks, insurance, and other income sources—not just one massive money pile.

One way to help shore up your income gaps is by working with your financial professional and a qualified tax advisor to help mitigate your tax exposure. If you have a 401(k) or IRA, a tax advisor in your corner may be able to help you figure out how and when to take distributions from your account in a way that doesn't push you into a higher tax bracket. Or you might learn how to use tax-advantaged bonds more effectively. Effective tax planning isn't necessarily about "adding" to your income. Especially regarding retirement, it's less about what you make than it is about what you keep. Paying a lower tax bill keeps more money in your pocket, which is where you want it when it comes to retirement income.

Now you can look at ways to cover your remaining retirement goals. Are there products like long-term care insurance specific to a certain kind of expense you anticipate? Is there a particular asset you want to use for your "play" money—money for trips and gifts for the grandkids? Is there any way you can portion off money for those charitable legacy plans?

Once you have analyzed your income wants, needs, and the assets to realistically cover them, you may have a gap. The masterstroke of a competent financial professional will be to help you figure out how you will cover that gap. Will you need to cut out a round of golf a week? Maybe skip the new car? Or will you need to take more substantial action?

One way to cover an income gap is to consider working longer or even part-time before retirement and even after that magical calendar date. This may not be the best "plan" for you; disabilities, work demands, and physical or emotional limitations can hinder the best-laid plans to continue working. However, if it is physically possible for you, this is one considerable way to help your assets last, for more than one reason.

In fact, 46 percent of the Americans responding to a survey report they plan to work part-time after retiring, while 18 percent indicated they planned to work past the age of seventy.[29]

When I first started to help clients with financial planning, I worked with many state employees such as teachers, police officers, and firefighters.

What I found was interesting. They often brought documents denoting income streams and asked, with a degree of uncertainty, whether they could pull the trigger and retire.

On occasion, I could point to their projected Social Security and pension income streams and show them that they stood to make more in retirement than they did while working. In addition, some had substantial assets saved in a 403(b) plan.

It dawned on me that they were good at their jobs and good at accruing retirement savings they could reference. Yet they couldn't quite put all the pieces together and sometimes lacked confidence. After all, leaving the workforce and no longer receiving regular compensation or benefits can be an unsettling proposition for some. A fear of the unknown can surface when contemplating retirement.

I simply had to affirm their confidence in the retirement plan. And that, quite frankly, is often the question that concerns people most about retirement: Am I going to be okay?

---

[29] Palash Ghosh. Forbes.com. May 6, 2021. "A Third Of Seniors Seek To Work Well Past Retirement Age, Or Won't Retire At All, Poll Finds" https://www.forbes.com/sites/palashghosh/2021/05/06/a-third-of-seniors-seek-to-work-well-past-retirement-age-or-wont-retire-at-all-poll-finds/?sh=1d2ece836b95

When you're retired, you no longer have an employer paying you a steady check. It is up to you to make sure you have saved and planned for the income you need.

CHAPTER 5

Social Security

Social Security is often the foundation of retirement income. Backed by the strength of the U.S. Treasury, it provides perhaps the most dependable paycheck you will have in retirement.

From the time you collect your first paycheck from the job that made you a bona fide taxpayer (for me, it was bagging groceries at a Publix in Mandarin, Florida), you are paying into the grand old Social Security system. What grew and developed out of the pressures of the Great Depression has become one of the most popular government programs in the country, and, if you pay in for the equivalent of ten years or more, you, too, can benefit from the Social Security program.

Now, before we get into the nitty-gritty of Social Security, I'd like to address a current concern: Will Social Security still be there for you when you reach retirement age?

The Future of Social Security

This question is ever-present as headlines trumpet an underfunded Social Security program, alongside the sea of baby boomers retiring in droves and the comparatively smaller pool of younger people who are funding the system.

The Social Security Administration itself acknowledges this concern as each Social Security statement now contains a link to its website (ssa.gov) and a page entitled, "Will Social Security Be There For Me?"

Just a reminder, as if you needed one, that nothing in life is guaranteed. Additionally, depending on who you're listening to, Social Security funds may run low before 2034 thanks to the financial instability and government spending that accompanied the 2020 COVID-19 pandemic.

Before you get too discouraged, though, here are a few thoughts to keep you going:

- Even if the program is only paying 78 cents on the dollar for scheduled benefits, 78 percent is notably not zero.

- The Social Security Administration has made changes in the distant and near past to protect the fund's solvency, including increasing retirement ages and striking certain filing strategies.

- There are many changes Congress could make, and lawmakers routinely discuss how to fix the system, such as further increasing full retirement age and eligibility.

- One thing no one is seriously discussing? Reneging on current obligations to retirees or the soon-to-retire.

Take heart. The real answer to the question, "Will Social Security be there for me?" is still yes.

This question is important to consider when you look at how much we, as a nation, rely on this program. Did you know Social Security benefits replace about 40 percent of a person's original income when they retire?[30]

If you ask me, that's a pretty significant piece of your retirement income puzzle.

Another caveat? You may not realize this, but no one can legally "advise" you about your Social Security benefits.

---

[30] ssa.gov. "Alternate Measure of Replacement Rates for Social Security Benefits and Retirement Income" https://www.ssa.gov/policy/docs/ssb/v68n2/v68n2p1.html.

"But, Bob," you may be thinking, "isn't that part of what you do? And what about that nice gentleman at the Social Security Administration office I spoke with on the phone?"

Don't get me wrong. Social Security Administration employees know their stuff. They are trained to understand policies and programs, and they are usually pretty quick to tell you what you can and cannot do. But the government specifically stipulates, because Social Security is a benefit you alone have paid into and earned, your Social Security decisions, too, are yours alone.

When it comes to financial professionals, we can't push you in any direction, but—there's a big but here—working with a well-informed financial professional is still incredibly handy for your Social Security decisions. Why? Because someone who's worth his or her salt will know what withdrawal strategies might pertain to your specific situation and will ask questions that can help you determine what you are looking for when it comes to your Social Security.

For instance, some people want the highest possible monthly benefit. Others want to start their benefits early, not always because of financial need. I heard about one man who called in to start his Social Security payments the day he qualified, just because he liked to think of it as the government paying back a debt it owed him, and he enjoyed the feeling of receiving a check from Uncle Sam.

Whatever your reasons, questions, or feelings regarding Social Security, the decision is yours alone; but working with a financial professional can help you put your options in perspective by showing you—both with industry knowledge and with proprietary software or planning processes— where your benefits fit into your overall strategy for retirement income.

One reason the federal government doesn't allow for "advice" related to Social Security, I suspect, is so no one can profit from giving you advice related to your Social Security benefit—or from providing any clarifications. Again, this is a sign of a good financial professional. Those who are passionate about their work will be knowledgeable about what benefit strategies might be to your advantage and will happily share those possible options with you.

Full Retirement Age

When it comes to Social Security, it seems like many people only think so far as "yes." They don't take the time to understand the various options available. Instead, because it is common knowledge you can begin your benefits at age sixty-two, that's what many of us do. While more people are opting to delay taking benefits, age sixty-two is still firmly the most popular age to start.[31]

What many people fail to understand is, by starting benefits early, they may be leaving a lot of money on the table. You see, the Social Security Administration bases your monthly benefit on two factors: your earnings history and your full retirement age (FRA).

From your earnings history, they pull the thirty-five years you made the most money and use a mathematical indexing formula to figure out a monthly average from those years. If you paid into the system for less than thirty-five years, then every year you didn't pay in will be counted as a zero.

Once they have calculated what your monthly earning would be at FRA, the government then calculates what to put on your check based on how close you are to FRA. FRA was originally set at sixty-five, but, as the population aged and lifespans lengthened, the government shifted FRA later and later, based on an individual's year of birth. Check out the following chart to see when you will reach FRA.[32]

---

[31] Chris Kissell. moneytalknews.com. January 20, 2021. "This Is When the Most People Start Taking Social Security." https://www.moneytalksnews.com/the-most-popular-age-for-claiming-social-security/

[32] Social Security Administration. "Full Retirement Age." https://www.ssa.gov/planners/retire/retirechart.html

Age to Receive Full Social Security Benefits*

(Called "full retirement age" [FRA] or "normal retirement age.")

Year of Birth*	FRA
1937 or earlier	65
1938	65 and 2 months
1939	65 and 4 months
1940	65 and 6 months
1941	65 and 8 months
1942	65 and 10 months
1943-1954	66
1955	66 and 2 months
1956	66 and 4 months
1957	66 and 6 months
1958	66 and 8 months
1959	66 and 10 months
1960 and later	67

If you were born on Jan. 1 of any year, you should refer to the previous year. (If you were born on the 1st of the month, we figure your benefit [and your full retirement age] as if your birthday was in the previous month.)

When you reach FRA, you are eligible to receive 100 percent of whatever the Social Security Administration says is your full monthly benefit.

Starting at age sixty-two, for every year before FRA you claim benefits, your monthly check is reduced by 5 percent or more. Conversely, for every year you delay taking benefits past FRA, your monthly benefit increases by 8 percent (until age seventy—after that, there is no monetary advantage to delaying Social Security benefits). While your circumstances and needs may vary, a lot of financial professionals still urge people to at least consider delaying until they reach age seventy.

Why wait?[33]

Taking benefits early could affect your monthly check by ______.								
62	63	64	65	66	FRA 67	68	69	70
-30%	-25%	-20%	-13.3%	-6.7%	0	+8%	+16%	+24%

[34]

My Social Security

If you are over age thirty, you have probably received a notice from the Social Security Administration telling you to activate something called "My Social Security." This is a handy way to learn more about your particular benefit options, to keep track of what your earnings record looks like, and to calculate the benefits you have accrued over the years.

Essentially, My Social Security is an online account you can activate to see what your personal Social Security picture looks

---

[33] Social Security Administration. April 2021. "Can You Take Your Benefits Before Full Retirement Age?"
https://www.ssa.gov/planners/retire/applying2.html
[34] Social Security Administration. 2023. "Effect of Early or Delayed Retirement on Retirement Benefits"
https://www.ssa.gov/oact/ProgData/ar_drc.html

like, which you can do at www.ssa.gov/myaccount. This can be extremely helpful when it comes to planning for income in retirement and figuring up the difference between your anticipated income versus anticipated expenses.

COLA

Social Security is a largely guaranteed piece of the retirement puzzle: If you get a statement that reads you should expect $1,000 a month, you can be sure you will receive $1,000 a month. But there is one variable detail, and that is something called the cost-of-living adjustment, or COLA.

The COLA is an increase in your monthly check meant to address inflation in everyday life. After all, your expenses will likely continue to experience inflation in retirement, but you will no longer have the opportunity for raises, bonuses, or promotions you had when you were working. Instead, Social Security receives an annual cost-of-living increase tied to the Department of Labor's Consumer Price Index for Urban Wage Earners and Clerical Workers, or CPI-W. If the CPI-W measurement shows inflation rose a certain amount for regular goods and services, then Social Security recipients will see that reflected in their COLA.

COLA adjustments have climbed as high as 14.3 percent (1980), and in 2023, they reached 8.7 percent — the largest increase in more than forty years. But in a no- or low-inflation environment (such as in 2010, 2011, and 2016), Social Security recipients will not receive an adjustment.[35] The 2024 adjustment decreased to 3.2 percent from 8.7 percent in 2023.[36] Some view the COLA as a perk, bump, or bonus, but, in reality, it works more like this: Your mom sends you to the store with $2.50 for a gallon of milk. Milk costs exactly $2.50. The next week, you go back with that same amount, but it is now

---

[35] ssa.gov. "Cost-Of-Living Adjustments" ssa.gov/oact/cola/colaseries.html
[36] ssa.gov. "Cost-of-Living Adjustment (COLA) Information for 2024" https://www.ssa.gov/cola/

$2.52 for a gallon, so you go back to Mom, and she gives you 2 cents. You aren't bringing home more milk—it just costs more money.

So the COLA is less about "making more money" and more about keeping seniors' purchasing power from eroding when inflation is a big factor, such as in 1975, when it was 8 percent![37] Still, don't let that detract from your enthusiasm about COLAs; after all, what if Mom's solution was: "Here's the same $2.50; try to find pennies from somewhere else to get that milk!"?

Spousal Benefits

We've talked about FRA, but another big Social Security decision involves spousal benefits.

If you or your spouse has a long stretch of zeros in your earnings history—perhaps if one of you stayed home for years, caring for children or sick relatives—you may want to consider filing for spousal benefits instead of filing on your own earnings history. A spousal benefit can be up to 50 percent of the primary wage earner's benefit at full retirement age.

To begin drawing a spousal benefit, you must be at least sixty-two years old, and the primary wage earner must have already filed for his or her benefit. While there are penalties for taking spousal benefits early, you cannot earn credits for delaying past full retirement age.[38]

As I wrote, the spousal benefit can be a big deal for those who don't have a very long pay history, but it's important to weigh your own earned benefits against the option of withdrawing based on a fraction of your spouse's benefits.

To look at how this could play out, let's use a hypothetical couple: Mary Jane, who is sixty, and Peter, who is sixty-two.

---

[37] Social Security Administration. "Cost-Of-Living Adjustment (COLA) Information for 2022." https://www.ssa.gov/cola/
[38] Social Security Administration. "Retirement Planner: Benefits For You As A Spouse." https://www.ssa.gov/planners/retire/applying6.html

Let's say Peter's benefit at FRA — in his case sixty-seven — would be $1,600. If Peter begins his benefits right now (five years before FRA), his monthly check will be $1,120. If Mary Jane begins taking spousal benefits in two years at the earliest date possible, her monthly benefits will be reduced to $392 per month (remember, at FRA, the most she can qualify for is half of Peter's FRA benefit).

What if Peter and Mary Jane both wait until FRA? At sixty-seven, Peter begins taking his full benefit of $1,600 a month. Two years later, when she reaches age sixty-seven, Mary Jane will qualify for $800 a month. By waiting until FRA, the couple's monthly benefit goes from $1,512 to $2,400.

What if Peter delays until age seventy to get his maximum possible benefit? For each year past FRA he delays, his monthly benefits increase by 8 percent. This means that at seventy, he could file for a monthly benefit of $1,984. However, delayed retirement credits do not affect spousal benefits, so as soon as Peter files at seventy, Mary Jane would also file (at age sixty-eight) for her maximum benefit of $800, so their highest possible combined monthly check is $2,784.[39]

Divorced Spouses

There are a few considerations for those of us who have gone through a divorce. If you 1) were married for ten years or more *and* 2) have since been divorced for at least two years *and* 3) are unmarried *and* 4) your ex-spouse qualifies to begin Social Security, you qualify for a spousal benefit based on your ex-husband or ex-wife's earnings history at FRA. A divorced spousal benefit is different from the married spousal benefit in

---

[39] Office of the Chief Actuary. Social Security Administration. "Social Security Benefits: Benefits for Spouses"
https://www.ssa.gov/OACT/quickcalc/spouse.html#calculator

one way: You don't have to wait for your ex-spouse to file before you can file yourself.[40]

For instance, Charles and Moira were married for fifteen years before their divorce, when he was thirty-six and she was forty. Moira has been remarried for twenty years, and, although Charles briefly remarried, his second marriage ended after a few years. Charles' benefits are largely calculated based on his many years of volunteering in schools, meaning his personal monthly benefit is close to zero.

Although Moira has deferred her retirement, opting to delay benefits until she is seventy, Charles can begin taking benefits calculated from Moira's work history at FRA as early as sixty-two. However, he will also have the option of waiting until FRA to collect the maximum, or 50 percent of Moira's earned monthly benefit at her FRA.

Widowed Spouses

If your marriage ended with the death of your spouse, you might claim a benefit for your spouse's earned income as his or her widow/widower, called a survivor's benefit. Unlike a spousal benefit or divorced benefits, if your husband or wife dies, you can claim his or her full benefit. Also, unlike spousal benefits, if you need to, you can begin taking income when you turn sixty. However, as with other benefit options, your monthly check will be permanently reduced for withdrawing benefits before FRA.

If your spouse began taking benefits before he or she died, you can't delay withdrawing your survivor's benefits to get delayed credits. The Social Security Administration maintains

---

[40] Social Security Administration. "Retirement Planner: If You Are Divorced." https://www.ssa.gov/planners/retire/divspouse.html

you can only get as much from a survivor's benefit as your deceased spouse might have received, had he or she lived.[41]

Taxes, Taxes, Taxes

With Social Security, as with everything, it is important to consider taxes. It may be surprising, but your Social Security benefits are not tax-free. Despite having been taxed to accrue those benefits in the first place, you may have to pay Uncle Sam income taxes on up to 85 percent of your Social Security.

The Social Security Administration figures these taxes using what they call "the provisional income formula." Your provisional income formula differs from the adjusted gross income you use for your regular income taxes. Instead, to find out how much of your Social Security benefit is taxable, the Social Security Administration calculates it this way:

Provisional Income = Adjusted Gross Income + Nontaxable Interest + ½ of Social Security

See that piece about nontaxable interest? That generally means interest from government bonds and notes. It surprises many people that, although you may not pay taxes on those assets, their income will count against you when it comes to Social Security taxation.

Once you have figured out your provisional income (also called "combined income"), you can use the following chart to figure out your Social Security taxes.[42]

---

41 Social Security Administration. "Social Security Benefit Amounts For The Surviving Spouse By Year Of Birth." https://www.ssa.gov/planners/survivors/survivorchartred.html
42 Social Security Administration. "Benefits Planner: Income Taxes and Your Social Security Benefits." https://www.ssa.gov/planners/taxes.html

Taxes on Social Security		
Provisional Income = Adjusted Gross Income + Nontaxable Interest + ½ of Social Security		
If you are ____ and your provisional income is____, then...		Uncle Sam will tax ___ of your Social Security
Single	Married, filing jointly	
Less than $25,000	Less than $32,000	0%
$25,000 to $34,000	$32,000 to $44,000	Up to 50%
More than $34,000	More than $44,000	Up to 85%

This is one more reason it may benefit you to work with financial and tax professionals. They can look at your entire financial picture to make your overall retirement plan as tax-efficient as possible—including your Social Security benefit.

Roth IRAs are tax-free income after age fifty-nine-and-a-half and the account is at least five years old. Consider converting some or all of your qualified retirement funds to a Roth if possible. It will require you to pay the income taxes due on these funds now, but they can be withdrawn in retirement tax free. You may be able to take the appropriate amount of income from tax-deferred and tax-free accounts to make your Supplemental Security Income (SSI) less (or not at all) taxable. If you reposition your assets into a tax-deferred vehicle like annuities or life insurance to help minimize tax exposure, you can possibly make your Social Security benefits more tax efficient.

Working and Social Security: The Earnings Test

If you haven't reached FRA, but you started your Social Security benefits and are still working, things get a little hairy.

Because you have started Social Security payments, the Social Security Administration will pay out your benefits (at that reduced rate, of course, because you haven't reached your FRA). Yet, because you are working, the organization must also withhold from your check to add to your benefits, which you are already collecting. See how this complicates matters?

To address the situation, the government has what is called the earnings test. For 2024, you can earn up to $22,320 without it affecting your Social Security check if you're younger than full retirement age. But, for every $2 you earn past that amount, the Social Security Administration will withhold $1. The earnings test loosens in the year of your FRA; if you are reaching FRA in 2024, you can earn up to $59,520 before you run into the earnings test, and the government only withholds $1 for every $3 past that amount.

The month you reach FRA, you are no longer subject to any earnings withholding. For instance, if you are still working and will turn sixty-seven on December 28, 2024, you would only have to worry about the earnings test until December, and then you can ignore it entirely. Keep in mind that the money the government withholds from your Social Security benefits while you are working before FRA will be tacked back onto your benefits check after FRA.[43]

When do I sometimes suggest that someone take their SSI? Generally, take it when you need it. I'd rather you take your SSI earlier in retirement and leave your assets alone. SSI isn't inheritable, but your assets are. SSI is also inflation-adjusted, so we can use it in the foundation of the "fiscal house."

---

43 Social Security Administration. "Receiving Benefits While Working" https://www.ssa.gov/benefits/retirement/planner/whileworking.html

CHAPTER 6

401(k)s & IRAs

Have you heard? Today's retirement is not your parents' retirement. You see, back in the day, it was pretty common to work for one company for the vast majority of your career and then retire with a gold watch and a pension.

The gold watch was a symbol of the quality time you had put in at that company, but the pension was more than a symbol. Instead, it was a guarantee—as solid as your employer—that they would repay your hard work with a certain amount of income in your old age. Did you see the caveat there? Your pension's guarantee was *as solid as your employer*. The problem was, what if your employer went under?

Companies that failed couldn't pay their retired employees' pensions, leading to financial challenges for many. Beginning in 1974 with Congress' passage of the Employee Retirement Income Security Act, federal legislation and regulations aimed at protecting retirees were everywhere. One piece of legislation included a relatively obscure section of the Internal Revenue Code, added in 1978. Section 401(k), to be specific.

IRC section 401, subsection k, created tax advantages for employer-sponsored financial products, even if the main contributor was the employee him or herself. Over the years, more employers took note, beginning an age of transition away from pensions and toward 401(k) plans. A 401(k) is a retirement account with certain tax benefits and restrictions on the investments or other financial products inside of it.

Essentially, 401(k)s and their individual retirement account (IRA) counterparts are "wrappers" that provide tax benefits around assets; typically, the assets that compose IRAs and 401(k)s are mutual funds, stock and bond mixes, and money market accounts. However, IRA and 401(k) contents are becoming more diverse these days, with some companies offering different kinds of annuity options within their plans.

Where pensions are defined-*benefit* plans, 401(k)s and IRAs are defined-*contribution* plans. The one-word change outlines the basic difference. Pensions spell out what you can expect to receive from the plan but not necessarily how much money it will take to fund those benefits. With 401(k)s, an employer sets a standard for how much they will contribute (if any), and you can be certain of what you are contributing. Still, there is no outline for what you can expect to receive in return for those contributions.

Modern employment looks very different. A 2022 survey by the Bureau of Labor Statistics determined U.S. workers stayed with their employers a median of 4.1 years. Workers ages fifty-five to sixty-four had a little more staying power and were most likely to stay with their employer for about ten years.[44] Participation in 401(k) plans has steadily risen this century, totaling $7.3 trillion in assets in 2021 compared to $3.1 trillion in 2011. The survey revealed about 60 million active participants engaged in 401(k) plans.[45]

Those statistics make it clear that 401(k) plans have replaced pensions at many companies and, for that matter, a gold watch.

---

[44] Bureau of Labor Statistics. September 22, 2022. "Employee Tenure Summary." https://www.bls.gov/news.release/tenure.nr0.htm

[45] Investment Company Institute. October 11, 2021. "Frequently Asked Questions About 401(k) Plan Research" https://www.ici.org/faqs/faq/401k/faqs_401k#:~:text=In%202020%2C%20there%20were%20about,of%20former%20employees%20and%20retirees.

A pension gives you options and helps create a solid foundation in your fiscal house. Company pensions often come with similar options. The highest payment option is usually a "single life" payment guaranteed for only the life of the retiree. A "joint life" payment is guaranteed for the life of the retiree and their spouse, but the payment amount is less than the single-life payment. There are also usually other options, such as guaranteed time periods and lump sum options. Many people choose to take the lump sum so they can take control of their assets or pass them to a beneficiary. However, we put the needs of our clients first while explaining the pros and cons of their pension choices.

If there is anything to learn from this paradigm shift, it's that you must look out for yourself. Whether you have worked for a company for two years or twenty, you are still the one who has to look out for your own best interests. That holds doubly true when it comes to preparing for retirement. If you are one of the lucky ones who still has a pension, good for you. But for the rest of us, it is likely a 401(k)—or possibly one of its nonprofit- or government-sector counterparts, a 403(b) or 457 plan—is one of your biggest assets for retirement.

Some employers offer incentives to contribute to their company plans, like a company match. On that subject, I have one thing to say: *Do it!* Nothing in life is free, as they say, but a company match on your retirement funds is about as close to free money as it gets. If you can make the minimum to qualify for your company's match at all, go for it.

Now, it's likely, during our working years, we mostly "set and forget" our 401(k) funding. Because it is tax-advantaged, your employer is taking money from your paycheck—before taxes— and putting it into your plan for you. Maybe you got to pick a selection of investments, or maybe your company only offers one choice of investment in your 401(k). Either way, while you are gainfully employed, your most impactful decision may just be the decision to continue funding your plan in the first place. But, when you are ready to retire or move jobs, you have choices to make requiring a little more thought and care.

When you are ready to part ways with your job, you have a few options:

- Leave the money where it is
- Take the cash (and pay income taxes and perhaps a 10 percent additional federal tax if you are younger than age fifty-nine-and-one-half)
- Transfer the money to another employer plan (if the new plan allows)
- Roll the money over into a self-directed IRA

Now, these are just general options. You will have to decide, hopefully with the help of a financial professional, what's right for you. For instance, 401(k)s are typically pretty closely tied to the companies offering them, so when changing jobs, it may not always be possible to transfer a 401(k) to another 401(k). Leaving the money where it is may also be out of the question—some companies have direct cash payout or rollover policies once someone is no longer employed.

Also, remember what we mentioned earlier about how we change jobs more often these days? That means you likely have a 401(k) with your current company, but you may also have a string of retirement accounts trailing you from other jobs.

People are busy. Most folks are also somewhat ambitious and seek new and better opportunities in their life. This may lead to them having multiple jobs during their working years with better earning potential or working environments. However, working at many different jobs throughout your life can have some unexpected consequences when preparing for retirement.

Occasionally when a new family comes into my office for the first time, I'll see they have multiple 401(k)s, 403(b)s, or IRA accounts from the various jobs they've had over the years. Leading up to retirement, this can be confusing because they get a pile of monthly statements from all these accounts, and they might not have a clear plan for any of them.

We help our clients discover they can often combine most, if not all, of these accounts into one single account. Similar to housekeeping, by pooling these accounts together, you create a more organized portfolio and, ideally, less stress. This combined account can now focus on its objectives.

When it comes to your retirement income, it's important to be able to pull together *all* your assets, so you can examine what you have and where, and then decide what you will do with it.

Tax-Qualified, Tax-Preferred, Tax-Deferred ... Still TAXED

Financial media often cite IRAs and 401(k)s for their tax benefits. After all, with traditional plans, you put your money in, pre-tax, and it hopefully grows for years, even decades, untaxed. That's why these accounts are called "tax-qualified" or "tax-deferred" assets. They aren't *tax-free!* Rarely does Uncle Sam allow business to continue without receiving his piece of the pie, and your retirement assets are no different. If you didn't pay taxes on the front end, you will pay taxes on the money you withdraw from these accounts in retirement. Don't get me wrong: This isn't an inherently good or bad thing; it's just the way it is. It's important to understand, though, for the sake of planning ahead.

In retirement, many people assume they will be in a lower tax bracket. Are you planning to pare down your lifestyle in retirement? Perhaps you are, and perhaps you will have substantially less income in retirement. But many of my clients tell me they want to live life more or less the same as they always have. The money they would previously have spent on business attire or gas for their commute they now want to spend on hobbies and grandchildren. That's all fine, and for many of them, it is doable, but does it put them in a lower tax bracket? Probably not.

Keep in mind, IRAs, 401(k)s, and their alternatives have a few limitations because of their special tax status. For one thing, the IRS sets limits on your contributions to these retirement accounts. If you are contributing to a 401(k) or an equivalent nonprofit or government plan, your annual contribution limit is $23,000 (as of 2024). If you are fifty or older, the IRS allows additional contributions, called "catch-up contributions," of up to $7,500 on top of the regular limit of $23,000. For an IRA, the limit is $7,000, with a catch-up limit of an additional $1,000.[46] Beginning in 2026, catch-up contributions for individuals with income exceeding $145,000 must transfer into a Roth IRA.[47]

Because their tax advantages come from their intended use as retirement income, withdrawing funds from these accounts before you turn fifty-nine-and-one-half can carry stiff penalties. In addition to fees your investment management company might charge, you will have to pay income tax *and* a 10 percent federal tax penalty, with few exceptions.

The fifty-nine-and-one-half rule for retirement accounts is incredibly important to remember, especially when you're young. Younger workers are often tempted to cash out an IRA from a previous employer and then are surprised to find their checks missing 20 percent of the account value to income taxes, penalty taxes, and account fees.

Many millennials I see in my practice say, while they may be socking money away in their workplace retirement plan, it is often the *only* place they are saving. This could be problematic later because of the fifty-nine-and-one-half rule; what if you have an emergency? It is important to fund your retirement, but you need to have some liquid assets handy as emergency funds. This can help you avoid breaking into your retirement accounts and incurring taxes and penalties because of the fifty-nine-and-one-half rule.

---

[46] Fidelity.com. November 2, 2023. "IRA contribution limits for 2022, 2023, and 2024" https://www.fidelity.com/learning-center/smart-money/ira-contribution-limits

[47] Robert Powell. thestreet.com. "Ask the Hammer: Catch-up Contributions Now Permitted Until 2026" https://www.thestreet.com/retirement-daily/ask-the-hammer/catch-up-contributions-now-permitted-until-2026

RMDs

Remember how we talked about the 401(k) or IRA being a "tax wrapper" for your funds? Well, eventually, Uncle Sam will want a bite of that candy bar. So, when you turn seventy-three, the government requires you withdraw a portion of your account, which the IRS calculates based on the size of your account and your estimated lifespan. This required minimum distribution, or RMD, is the government's insurance it will collect some taxes, at some point, from your earnings. Because you didn't pay taxes on the front end, you will now pay income taxes on whatever you withdraw, including your RMDs.

Let me reiterate something I pointed out in the Longevity chapter. Beginning at age seventy-three, you are required to withdraw a certain minimum amount every year from your 401(k) or IRA, or else you will face a tax penalty on any RMD monies you should have withdrawn but didn't—and that's on top of income tax. The SECURE Act 2.0 reduced the penalty to 25 percent (from 50 percent). Timely corrections also can reduce the penalty to 10 percent.[48]

Even after you begin RMDs, you can still also continue contributing to your 401(k) or IRAs if you are still employed, which can affect the whole discussion on RMDs and possible tax considerations. The SECURE Act 2.0 raised the RMD age to seventy-three from seventy-two. In addition, the latest legislation stipulates the RMD age will increase to seventy-five for those turning seventy-four after December 31, 2032.[49]

If you don't need income from your retirement accounts, RMDs can seem like more of a tax burden than an income boon. While some people prefer to reinvest their RMDs, this comes with the possibility of additional taxation: You'll pay income taxes on your RMDs and then potential capital gains taxes on

---

[48] Jim Probasco. Investopedia.com. January 6, 2023. "SECURE 2.0 Act of 2022." https://www.investopedia.com/secure-2-0-definition-5225115
[49] Ibid.

the growth of your investments. If you are legacy-minded, there are other ways to use RMDs, many of which have tax benefits.

SECURE Act 2.0 provisions

In addition to changes imposed for RMD ages, Secure Act 2.0 also expanded access to retirement savings using different methods. Provisions in the legislation go into effect at different times, ranging from 2023-25.

- Beginning January 2, 2024, plan participants can access up to $1,000 (once a year) from retirement savings for emergency personal or family expenses without paying a 10 percent early withdrawal penalty.
- Beginning January 2, 2024, employees can establish a Roth emergency savings account of up to $2,500 per participant.
- Beginning January 2, 2024, domestic abuse survivors can withdraw the lesser of $10,000 or 50 percent of their retirement account without penalty.
- Beginning January 1, 2023, victims of a qualified, federally declared disaster can withdraw up to $22,000 from their retirement account without penalty.[50]

One of the most important developments stemming from the SECURE Act and SECURE Act 2.0 proved, in my opinion, to be an affirmation from Congress regarding America's debt situation. The legislation essentially eliminated the Stretch IRA for most non-spousal beneficiaries. The Stretch IRA made it possible to minimize IRA withdrawals over the length of a beneficiaries' life.

With passage of these measures, inherited retirement RMD distribution periods changed to ten years for many beneficiaries. Previously, those distributions could be spread over the lifetime of a beneficiary. Spouses, and certain others

---

[50] Betterment.com. January 12, 2023. "SECURE Act 2.0: Signed into Law" https://www.betterment.com/work/resources/secure-act-2

are exempt from the new rule and can still take advantage of the Stretch IRA provision.

For those who are not exempt, however, like most adult children who are beneficiaries of a conventional IRA, the IRS collects its portion of money over a shorter, ten-year period of time. Understand that if a person passes away in their eighties or nineties, which is common considering today's longevity data, they will pass away their wealth to adult children who are likely in their fifties and sixties. For those beneficiaries in that age range, that period is often considered their maximum earning years. The federal government (IRS) collects money over a shorter period and during a time when the beneficiaries could be in the highest tax bracket of their careers.

Based on that prospect, the enactment of SECURE Act measures typically allows the government to condense the collection of taxes over a ten-year window. It is my opinion that the legislation eliminating the Stretch IRA for some beneficiaries was a move designed to offset deficit spending. At our company, we find it important to stay abreast of legislation that can potentially change rules associated with retirement planning.

Permanent Life Insurance

One way to turn those pesky RMDs into a legacy is through permanent life insurance. Assuming you need the death benefit coverage and can qualify for it medically, if properly structured, these products can pass on a sizeable death benefit to your beneficiaries, tax-free, as part of your general legacy plan.

ILIT

Another way to use RMDs toward your legacy is to work with an estate planning attorney to create an irrevocable life insurance trust (ILIT). This is basically a permanent life insurance policy placed within a trust. Because the trust is irrevocable, you would relinquish control of it, but, unlike with just a permanent life insurance policy, your death benefit won't count toward your taxable estate.

Annuities

Because annuities can be tax-deferred, using all or a portion of your RMDs to fund an annuity contract can be one way to further delay taxation while guaranteeing your income payments (either to you or your loved ones) later. Of course, this assumes you don't need the RMD income during your retirement.

Qualified Charitable Distributions

If you are charity-minded, you may use your RMDs toward a charitable organization instead of using them for income. You must do this directly from your retirement account (you can't take the RMD check and *then* pay the charity) for your withdrawals to be qualified charitable distributions (QCDs), but this is one way of realizing some of the benefits of a charitable legacy during your own lifetime. You will not need to pay taxes on your QCDs, and they won't count toward your annual charitable tax deduction limit, plus you'll be able to see how the organization you are supporting uses your donations. You should consult a financial professional on how to correctly make a QCD.

Most of the individuals and families we work with usually have the vast majority of their wealth saved inside of a 401(k), which is a wonderful vehicle for saving and growing money throughout a consumer's working years. The problem with 401(k) plans is most of them are tax-deferred, meaning the tax on the amount saved and the growth of the account have never seen one penny of taxes. This can create a "tax time bomb," as we refer to it, because when you want to begin using your 401(k) money in retirement, every penny you withdraw and spend will be taxable.

What's the problem with that? Well, decades ago, when my clients initially signed up for a 401(k) with their past employer, many were told they would be in a lower tax environment when they retired, so it's a good idea to defer those taxes until then. Well, fast forward thirty years or so later, and often, they have a large sum of money saved for retirement but realize they probably won't be in a better tax position. Your tax environment is predicated on the annual income you make, regardless of if it's from a job or a withdrawal from the 401(k). Most families we work with want to have a smooth transition into retirement and continue living the same general lifestyle they've become accustomed to, along with maintaining the same amount of income they're accustomed to. Thus, their tax situation doesn't improve—it can actually be worse in retirement.

Another problem with 401(k) accounts (or any tax-deferred accounts) is they eventually have a required minimum distribution (RMD). Basically, this means regardless of *if* you want to take a taxable distribution from your account, you are *required* to take money from the account once you're a certain age. These RMDS can easily be thousands of dollars, and for those high net worth individuals, could potentially amount to six figures that they are required to withdraw and be taxed on.

Roth IRA

Since the Taxpayer Relief Act of 1997, there has been a different kind of retirement account, or "tax wrapper," available to the public: the Roth. Roth IRAs and Roth 401(k)s each differ from their traditional counterparts in one big way: You pay your taxes on the front end. This means, once your post-tax money is in the Roth account, as long as you follow the rules and limitations of that account, your distributions are truly tax-free. You won't pay income tax when you take withdrawals, so, in turn, you don't have to worry about RMDs. However, Roth accounts have the same limitations as traditional 401(k)s and IRAs when it comes to withdrawing money before age fifty-nine-and-one-half, with the added stipulation that the account must have been open for at least five years in order for the account holder to make withdrawals.

I often tell my daughters, "Don't leave money on the table" – this is just another way of saying to make sure you seize every opportunity given to you in life. I apply the same principle when conferring with clients about taxation. Given income and taxable accounts, the tax code may present certain opportunities in a given year to have those accounts taxed at a lower rate than they may be in the future. Basically, we know that taxes hurt sometimes, but we're opting for less pain now versus more pain in the future. One example of this is by utilizing a concept called Roth IRA conversions.

There is an easy way to calculate how many years it will take for your money to double. It's called "The Rule of 72". If you divide the number seventy-two by the interest rate you expect to make, the result will be the number of years it will take for your investment to double. For example, if you make 7.2 percent in a stock market account (a rate some people would contend is fairly reasonable), your money will double in ten years. This is an important concept when it comes to your pre-tax accounts such as IRAs, pre-tax 401(k)s, 403(b)s, etc. The longer those accounts defer taxes, the larger the pre-tax amount may escalate. Hence, a larger amount of taxes will be due in the future.

As if that presumptive burden is not enough, most of my clients agree that tax brackets will increase in the future. So unless we do something about it now, we'll likely have larger accounts taxed at higher rates in the future. Drawing again from what I tell my daughters, don't leave money on the table. Seize your opportunities.

Enter the Roth IRA conversion.

As an example, let's assume Henry (fictional character) has approximately $3 million in pre-tax 401(k) accounts at the age of sixty-three. He realizes that he will be obligated to take his first required minimum distribution (RMD) in twelve years. At that point, the RMD age will have raised to seventy-five from seventy-three in accordance with stipulations approved in SECURE Act 2.0.

About 3.7 percent of Henry's account balance would presumably be withdrawn due to the mandatory RMD. Henry did the math: $3 million, multiplied by 0.037 (the 3.7 percent withdrawal percentage), would result in a $111,000 RMD. This, of course, does not thrill Henry. He wants to know, as Paul Harvey once put it on his nationally syndicated radio show, "the rest of the story."

If his 401(k) account would continue to be invested for the next ten years, using "The Rule of 72" and projecting a 7 percent rate of return, his account would nearly double. That meant his RMD would not be $113,000. Instead, using the projected $6 million balance, Henry would owe $226,000 for his first RMD.

Again, this does not thrill Henry, though it does signify an opportunity to use Roth IRA conversions. Each year before he turns seventy-five, he can convert more funds using Roth IRA conversions. Although he must pay taxes on the conversions, he can, in all likelihood, pay those taxes using a lower tax bracket and will not have a compounding tax issue created by a higher 401(k) account balance in the future.

With Roth IRA conversions, Henry could choose to convert all or a portion of his pre-tax account to a Roth IRA. Once the taxes get paid, and the account gets converted into a Roth, it will never be taxed again and will not have a required minimum distribution in his lifetime. In addition, he may be able to convert the account at a lower tax bracket now versus what we assumed the rates would be in the future. This could save Henry tens of thousands, or even hundreds of thousands, in future taxes.

A question arises, however. How can consumers ensure they don't convert too much in a given year and thrust themselves into an unnecessarily high tax bracket? What about other circumstances that can arise with Roth conversions, such as an IRMAA (income-related monthly adjustment amount) increasing the amount of your Medicare Part B and D premiums, thus increasing the amount your Social Security will be taxed?

At our office, we utilize tax planning software, which allows us to run different scenarios of Roth IRA conversions. These scenarios tell us how much in taxes will be due, the tax brackets of the conversions, and the potential "traps" that could materialize with the conversions. It allows us to recognize and seize opportunities while filling any "gaps" we see. In other words, don't leave money on the table.

Taking Charge

As mentioned earlier, the 401(k) and IRA have largely replaced pensions, but they aren't an equal trade.

Pensions are employer-funded; the money feeding into them is money that wouldn't ever show up on your pay stub. Because 401(k)s are self-funded, you must actively and consciously save. This distinction has made a difference when it comes to funding retirement. Fidelity Investments published a story detailing that the average 401(k) balance for a person age fifty-five to sixty-four is $189,800, but the median likely tells the full story. The median 401(k) balance for a person age fifty-five to sixty-four is $56,450. Those figures reflect Fidelity accounts from the third quarter of 2022.[51]

There can be many reasons why people underfund their retirement plans, like being overwhelmed by the investment choices or taking withdrawals from IRAs when they leave an employer. Still, the reason at the top of the list is this: People simply aren't participating to begin with.

So, whether you use a 401(k) with an employer or an IRA alternative with a private company, separate from your workplace, the most important retirement savings decision you

---

[51] Arielle O'Shea. Nerd Wallet. December 22, 2022. "The Average 401(k) Balance by Age" https://www.nerdwallet.com/article/investing/the-average-401k-balance-by-age

can make is to sock away your money somewhere in the first place.

CHAPTER 7

Annuities

In my practice, I offer my clients a variety of products—from securities to insurance—all designed to help them work toward their financial goals. You may be wondering: Why single out a single product in this book?

Well, while most of my clients have a pretty good understanding of business and finance, I sometimes find those who have the impression there must be magic involved. Some people assume there is a magic finance wand we can wave to change years' worth of savings into a strategy for retirement income. But it's not as easy as a goose laying golden eggs or the Fairy Godmother turning a pumpkin into a coach!

Finances aren't magic; it takes lots of hard work and, typically, several financial products and strategies to pull together a complete retirement plan. Of all the financial products I work with, it seems people find none more mysterious than annuities. And, if I may say, even some of those who recognize the word "annuity" have a limited understanding of the product. So, in the interest of demystifying annuities, let me tell you a little about what an annuity is.

In general, insurance is a financial hedge against risk. Car owners buy auto insurance to protect their finances in case they injure someone or someone injures them. Homeowners have house insurance to protect their finances in case of a fire, flood, or another disaster. People have life insurance to protect their finances in case of untimely death. Almost juxtaposed to life insurance, people have annuities in case of a long life; annuities can give you financial protection by providing consistent and reliable income payments.

The basic premise of an annuity is you, the annuitant, pay an insurance company some amount in exchange for their contractual guarantee they will pay you income for a certain time period. How that company pays you, for how long, and how much they offer are all determined by the annuity contract you enter into with the insurance company.

I often have families come into our office with pre-conceived negative opinions on annuities. They've usually heard these opinions on the TV or radio from some well-known personality who may not even be licensed to sell annuities, much less securities or any other financial products. When I hear this sentiment, I usually respond with, "Yes, there are some annuities I don't like either. I'm curious—what don't you like about annuities?" They often don't have any idea how to respond because they're just regurgitating what they've heard: Hate all annuities because they're bad *all* the time.

This is obviously nonsense. I find the problem often isn't with annuities themselves—often it's with how an annuity is used in the overall financial plan. However, when used correctly in a comprehensive financial plan, annuities can be good tools for wealth accumulation or as a consistent income stream. As with most successful retirement strategies, there *must* be a purpose behind what you're doing. Annuities can be a valuable option to help you accomplish your goals.

How You Get Paid

There are two ways for an annuity contract to provide income: The first is through what is called annuitization, and the second is through the use of income riders. We'll get into income riders in a bit, but let's talk about annuitization. That nice, long word is, in my opinion, one reason annuities have a reputation for mystery and misinformation.

Annuitization

When someone "annuitizes" a contract, it is the point where he or she turns on the income stream. Once a contract has been annuitized, there is no going back. With annuities, if the policyholder lives longer than the insurance company planned, the insurance company is still obligated to pay him or her, even if the payments end up being way more than the contract's actual value. If, however, the policyholder dies an untimely death, depending on the contract type, the insurance company may keep anything left of the money that funded the annuity—nothing would be paid out to the contract holder's survivors. You see where that could make some people balk? Now, modern annuities rarely rely on annuitization for the income portion of the contract, and instead have so many bells and whistles that the old concept of annuitization seems outdated, but because this is still an option, it's important to at least understand the basic concept.

Riders

Speaking of bells and whistles, let's talk about riders. Modern annuities have a lot of different options these days, many in the form of riders you can add to your contract for a fee—usually about 1 percent of the contract value per year. Each rider has its particulars, and the types of riders available will vary by the type of annuity contract purchased, but I'll just briefly outline some of these little extras:

- Lifetime income rider: Contract guarantees you an enhanced or flexible income for life
- Death benefit rider: Contract pays an enhanced death benefit to your beneficiaries even if you have annuitized
- Return of premium rider: Guarantees you (or your beneficiaries) will at least receive back the premium value of the annuity

- Long-term care rider: Provides a certain amount, sometimes as much as twice the normal income benefit amount for a period of time to help pay for long-term care if the contract holder is moved to a nursing home or assisted living situation

This isn't an extensive look, and usually the riders have fancier names based on the issuing company, like "Lorem Ipsum Insurance Company Income Preferred Bonus Fixed Index Annuity rider," but I just wanted to show you what some of the general options are in layperson's terms.

Types of Annuities

Annuities break down into four basic types: immediate, variable, fixed, and fixed index.

Immediate

Immediate annuities primarily rely on annuitization to provide income—you give the insurance company a lump sum up front, and your payments begin immediately. Once you begin receiving income payments, the transaction is irreversible, and you no longer have access to your money in a lump sum. When you die, any remaining contract value is typically forfeited to the insurance company.

All other annuity contract types are "deferred" contracts, meaning you fund your policy as a lump sum or over a period of years and you give it the opportunity to grow over time— sometimes years, sometimes decades.

Variable

A variable annuity is an insurance contract as well as an investment. It's sold by insurance companies, but only through someone who is registered to sell investment products. With a variable annuity contract, the insurance company invests your premiums in subaccounts that are tied to the stock market. This makes it a bit different from the other annuity contract types because it is the only contract where your money is subject to losses because of market declines. Your contract value has a greater opportunity to grow, but it also stands to lose. Additionally, your contract's value will be subject to the underlying investment's fees and limitations—including taxes, management fees, etc. Once it is time for you to receive income from the contract, the insurance company will pay you a certain income, locked in at whatever your contract's value was.

Variable annuities can involve higher fees, and many people have no idea they're sometimes paying an additional 3 to 4 percent or more in fees.

Fixed

A traditional fixed annuity is pretty straightforward. You purchase a contract with a guaranteed interest rate and, when you are ready, the insurance company will make regular income payments to you at whatever payout rate your contract guarantees. Those payments will continue for the rest of your life and, if you choose, for the remainder of your spouse's life.

Fixed annuities don't typically offer significant upside potential, but many people like them for their guarantees (after all, if your Aunt May lives to be ninety-five, knowing she has a paycheck later in life can be her mental and financial safety net), as well as for their predictability. Unlike variable annuities, which are subject to market risk and might be up one year and down the next, you can easily calculate the value of your fixed annuity over your lifetime.

Fixed Index

To recap, variable annuities take on more risk to offer more possibilities to grow. Fixed annuities have less potential growth, but they protect your principal. In the last couple of decades, many insurance companies have retooled their product line to offer fixed index annuities, which are sort of midway between variable and fixed annuities on that risk/reward spectrum. Fixed index annuities offer greater growth potential than traditional fixed annuities but less than variable annuities. Like traditional fixed annuities, however, fixed index annuities are protected from downside market losses.

Fixed index annuities earn interest that is tied to an external market index, meaning that, instead of your contract value growing at a set interest rate like a traditional fixed annuity, it has the potential to grow within a range. Your contract's value is credited interest based on the performance of an external market index like the S&P 500 while never being invested in the market itself. You can't invest in the S&P 500 directly, but each year, your annuity as the potential to earn interest based on the chosen index's performance, subject to limits set by the company such as caps, spreads, and participation rates.

For instance, if your contract caps your interest at 5 percent, then in a year that the S&P 500 gains 3 percent, your annuity value increases 3 percent. If the S&P 500 gains 35 percent, your annuity value gets a 5 percent interest bump. But since your money isn't actually invested in the market with a fixed index annuity, if the market nosedives (such as happened during 2000, 2008, 2020, and 2022, anyone?) you won't see any increase in your contract value. Conversely, there will also be no decrease in your contract value—no matter how badly the market performed, as long as you follow the terms of the contract, you won't lose any of the interest you were credited in previous years.

So, what if the S&P 500 shows a market loss of 30 percent? Your contract value isn't going anywhere (unless you purchased an optional rider—this charge will still come out of your annuity value each year). For those who are more interested in protection than growth potential, fixed index annuities can be an attractive option because, when the stock market has a long period of positive performance, a fixed index annuity can enjoy conservative growth. And, during stretches where the stock market is erratic and stock values across the board take significant losses? Fixed index annuities won't lose anything due to the stock market volatility.

Other Things to Know About Annuities

We just talked about the four kinds of annuity contracts available, but all of them have some commonalities as annuities.

For all annuities, the contractual guarantees are only as strong as the insurance company that sells the product, which makes it important to thoroughly check the credit ratings of any company whose products you are considering.

Annuities are tax-deferred, meaning you don't have to pay taxes on interest earnings each year as the contract value grows. Instead, you will pay ordinary income taxes on your withdrawals. These are meant to be long-term products, so, like other tax-deferred or tax-advantaged products, if you begin taking withdrawals from your contract before age fifty-nine-and-one-half, you may also have to pay a 10 percent federal tax penalty. Also, while annuities are generally considered illiquid, most contracts allow you to withdraw up to 10 percent of your contract value every year. Withdraw any more, however, and you could incur additional surrender penalties.

Keep in mind, your withdrawals will deplete the accumulated cash value, death benefit, and, possibly, the rider values of your contract.

Annuities aren't for everyone, but it's important to understand them before saying "yea" or "nay" on whether they fit into your plan; otherwise, you're not operating with complete information, wouldn't you agree? Regardless, you should talk to a financial professional who can help you understand annuities, help you dissect your particular financial needs, and help show you whether an annuity is appropriate for your retirement income plan.

CHAPTER 8

Estate & Legacy

In my practice, I devote a significant portion of my time to matters of estates. That doesn't mean drawing up wills or trusts or putting together powers of attorney or anything like that. After all, I'm not an estate planning attorney. But I am a financial professional, and what part of the "estate" isn't affected by money matters?

I've included this chapter because I have seen many people do estate planning wrong. Clients, or clients' families, have come in after experiencing a death in the family and have found themselves in the middle of probate, high taxes, or a discovery of something unforeseen (often long-term care) draining the estate.

I have also seen people do estate planning right: clients or families who visit my office to talk about legacies and how to make them last and adult children who have room to grieve without an added burden of unintended costs, without stress from a family ruptured because of inadequate planning.

I'll share some of these stories here. However, I'm not going to give you specific advice, since everyone's situation is unique. I only want to give you some things to think about and to underscore the importance of planning ahead.

We refer clients to two different types of attorneys with whom our company maintains strategic partnerships. The first is an estate planning attorney. They will help people execute wills, powers of attorneys, and even trusts if necessary.

An elder law attorney is a second type of attorney we recommend through our firm's strategic partnerships. This professional can help with legal matters associated with long-term care, Medicare and Medicaid, and help people navigate complexities and issues that can arise with elder care.

We have developed strong relationships through the strategic partnerships we have forged with attorneys we recommend. Nonetheless, we typically tell clients to speak with multiple estate planning or elder care attorneys before making a decision regarding services.

You Can't Take It With You

When it comes to legacy and estate planning, the most important thing is to *do it*. I have heard people from clients to celebrities (rap artist Snoop Dogg comes to mind) say they aren't interested in what happens to their assets when they die because they'll be dead. That's certainly one way to look at it. But I think that's a very selfish way to go about things—we all have people and causes we care about, and those who care about us. Even if the people we love don't *need* what we leave behind, they can still be fined or legally tied up in the probate process or burial costs if we don't plan for those. And that's not even considering what happens if you become incapacitated at some point while you are still alive. Having a plan in place can greatly reduce the stress of those responsibilities on your loved ones; it's just a loving thing to do.

Documents

There are a few documents that lay the groundwork of legacy planning. You've probably heard of all or most of them, but I'd like to review what they are and how people commonly use them. These are all things you should talk about with an estate planning attorney to establish your legacy.

Powers of Attorney

A power of attorney, or POA, is a document giving someone the authority to act on your behalf and in your best interests. These come in handy in situations where you cannot be present (think a vacation where you get stuck in Canada) or, for durable powers of attorney, even when you are incapacitated (think in a coma or coping with dementia).

It is important to have powers of attorney in place and to appoint someone you trust to act on your behalf in these matters. Have you ever heard of someone who was incapacitated after a car accident, whether from head trauma or being in a coma for weeks—sometimes months? Do you think their bills stopped coming due during that time? I like my phone company and my bank, but neither one is about to put a moratorium on sending me bills, particularly not for an extended or interminable period. A power of attorney would have the authority to pay your mortgage or cancel your cable while you are unable.

You can have multiple POAs and require them to act jointly.

What this looks like: Do you think two heads are better than one? One man, Chris, significantly relied on his two sons' opinions for both his business and personal matters. He appointed both sons as joint POA, requiring both their signoffs for his medical and financial matters.

You can have multiple POAs who can act independently.

What this looks like: Irene had three children with whom she routinely stayed. They lived in different areas of the country, which she thought was an advantage; one month she might be hiking out West, the next she could enjoy the newest off-Broadway production, and the next she could soak up some Southern sun. She named her three children as independently authorized POAs, so, if something happened, no matter where she was, the child closest could step in to act on her behalf.

You can have POAs who have different responsibilities.

What this looks like: Although Luke's friend Claire, a nurse, was his go-to and POA for health-related issues, financial matters usually made her nervous, so he appointed his good neighbor, Matt, as his POA in all of his financial and legal matters.

In addition to POAs, it may be helpful to have an advanced medical directive. This is a document where you have pre-decided what choices you would make about different health scenarios. An advanced medical directive can help ease the burden for your medical POA and loved ones, particularly when it comes to end-of-life care.

Wills

Perhaps the most basic document of legacy planning, a will is a legal document wherein you outline your wishes for your estate. When it comes to your estate after your death, having a will is the foundation of your legacy. Without one, your loved ones are left behind, guessing what you would have wanted, and the court will likely split your assets according to the state's defaults. Maybe that's exactly what you wanted, as far as anyone knows, right? Because even if you told your nephew he could have your car he's been driving, if it's not in writing, it still might go to the brother, sister, son, or daughter to whom you aren't speaking.

However, it may not be enough just to have a will. Even with a will, your assets will be subject to probate. Probate is what we call the state's process for determining a will's validity. A judge will go through your will to question if it conflicts with state law, if it is the most up-to-date document, if you were mentally competent at the time it was in order, etc. For some, this is a quick, easily-resolved process. For others, particularly if someone steps forward to contest the will, it may take years to settle, all the while subjecting the assets to court costs and attorney's fees.

One other undesirable piece of the probate process is that it is a public process. That means anyone can go to the courthouse, ask for copies of the case, and discover your assets. They can also see who is slated to receive what and who is disputing.

I believe that it's a good idea for everyone to consider having a will. It doesn't prevent someone's estate from going to probate, but it does make a judge's job much easier when directions for how to handle an estate are legally structured in writing. It dictates precisely what should happen with a person's assets upon their death and helps avert disputes among loved ones.

Be aware, however, that sometimes difficulties can arise without any kind of family dispute over beneficiary lines.

Consider this hypothetical situation. A couple without much in terms of assets—we'll call them Bruce and Evelyn—inherited $800,000 after the passing of Bruce's sister. Much of the money was in a 401(k) containing a deferred tax liability.

Much of the inheritance was placed in a beneficiary IRA in Bruce's name. The couple also put some of the money into an annuity. Finally, roughly $150,000 was placed in the bank in money market accounts, savings accounts, and certificates of deposit. All those accounts were established in Bruce's name. Evelyn had no access.

For about three years, the couple made out fine but never thought to put Evelyn's name on the accounts for joint access. Bruce, unfortunately, was diagnosed with a fast-spreading form of cancer and died suddenly. Evelyn was left to pay for funeral expenses, as well as household bills, but could not immediately access any of the couple's money.

While her name was on the annuity, a week or two would be required to access any of those funds. An investment account established from the couple's inheritance was in Bruce's name.

A death certificate and claim form would need to be executed before Evelyn could access those funds. Also, everything at the bank was in Bruce's name.

Evelyn eventually borrowed money from her sister to cover the cost of the funeral expenses. A time of sorrow also became a time of financial frustration and embarrassment simply because Evelyn did not have quick access to the couple's funds.

It's important to remember beneficiary lines trump wills. So, that large life insurance policy? What if, when you bought it fifteen years ago, you wrote your ex-husband's name on the beneficiary line? Even if you stipulate otherwise in your will, the company that holds your policy will pay out to your ex-spouse. Or, how about the thousands of dollars in your IRA you dedicated to the children thirty years ago, but one of your children was killed in a car accident, leaving his wife and two toddlers behind? That IRA is going to transfer to your remaining children, with nothing for your daughter-in-law and grandchildren.

That may paint a grim portrait, but I can't underscore enough the importance of working with a skilled estate planning attorney to keep your will and beneficiary lines up to date as your life changes.

During my years growing up in Jacksonville, I vividly remember going to Kingsley Lake, which featured a water park operated by the family that owned that prime property spread across forty acres. My favorite activity was sliding or jumping from a large dock into the water.

When the owner of the property passed away, it became known that he did not have an estate plan to cover expenses his loved ones would incur. The park was appraised for about $4 million dollars, but when an inheritance tax was assessed, the owner's adult children had roughly nine months to come up with about $1.5 million. They didn't possess that kind of money and liquidated the property, selling it for far less than its value.

Proper estate planning could have allowed the family to avoid that situation and pay the inheritance tax. Sadly, the park closed and all any of us have are fond memories of a summertime staple the family couldn't retain after their father's death.

Trusts

Another piece of legacy planning to consider is the trust.

A trust is set up through an attorney and allows a third party, or trustee, to hold your assets and determine how they will pass to your beneficiaries. Many people are skeptical of trusts because they assume trusts are only appropriate for the fabulously wealthy.

However, a simple trust will likely cost more than $1,000 if prepared by an attorney and fees can be higher for couples.[52] But a trust can help you avoid both the expense and publicity of probate, provide a more immediate transfer of wealth, avoid some taxes, and provide you greater control over your legacy.

For instance, if you want to set aside some funds for a grandchild's college education, you can make it a requirement he or she enrolls in classes before your trust will dispense any funds. Like a will, beneficiary lines will override your trust conditions, so you must still keep insurance policies and other assets up to date.

Like any financial or legal consideration, there are many options these days beyond the simple "yes or no" question of whether to have a trust. For one thing, you will need to consider if you want your trust to be revocable (you can change the terms while you are alive) or irrevocable (can't be changed; you are no longer the "owner" of the contents). A brief note here about irrevocable trusts: Although they have significant and greater tax benefits, they are still subject to a Medicaid look-back period. This means, if you transfer your assets into an irrevocable trust in an attempt to shelter them from a Medicaid

---

[52] Rickie Houston. smartasset.com. August 31, 2022. "How Much Does It Cost to Set Up a Trust? https://smartasset.com/estate-planning/how-much-does-it-cost-to-set-up-a-trust

spend-down, you will be ineligible for Medicaid coverage of long-term care for five years. Yet, an irrevocable trust can avoid both probate and estate taxes, and it can even protect assets from legal judgments against you.

Another thing to remember when it comes to trusts, in general, is, even if you have set up a trust, you must remember to fund it. Since becoming a financial professional in 2009 and an independent advisor since 2017, I've had numerous clients come to me, assuming they have protected their assets with a trust. When we talk about taxes and other pieces of their legacy, it turns out they never retitled any assets or changed any paperwork on the assets they wanted in the trust. So, please remember, a trust is just a bunch of fancy legal papers if you haven't followed through on retitling your assets.

Taxes

Although charitable contributions, trusts, and other tax-efficient strategies can reduce your tax bill, it's unlikely your estate will be passed on entirely tax-free. Yet, when it comes to building a legacy that can last for generations, taxes can be one of the heaviest drains on the impact of your hard work.

For 2024, the federal estate exemption was $13.61 million per individual and $27.22 million for a married couple, with estates facing up to a 40 percent tax rate after that.[53] Currently, the new estate limits are set to increase with inflation until January 1, 2026, when they will "sunset" back to the inflation-adjusted 2017 limits.[54] And that's not taking into account the various state regulations and taxes regarding estate and inheritance transfers.

Another tax concern "frequent flyer": retirement accounts.

---

[53] Katelyn Washington. Kiplinger.com. November 15, 2023. "Estate Tax Exemption Amount Increases for 2024"
https://www.kiplinger.com/taxes/estate-tax-exemption-amount-increases
[54] IRS.gov. December 20, 2022. "What's New — Estate and Gift Tax"
https://www.irs.gov/businesses/small-businesses-self-employed/whats-new-estate-and-gift-tax

Your IRA or 401(k) can be a source of tax issues when you pass away. For one thing, taking funds from a sizeable account can trigger a large tax bill. However, if you leave the assets in the account, there are still required minimum distributions (RMDs), which will take effect even after you die. If you pass the account to your spouse, he or she can keep taking your RMDs as is, or your spouse can retitle the account in his or her name and receive RMDs based on his or her life expectancy. Remember, if you don't take your RMDs, the IRS will take up to 25 percent of your required distribution (10 percent if corrections are made in a timely fashion), You will still have to pay income taxes whenever you withdraw that money. Provisions in the original SECURE Act, anyone who inherits your IRA, with few exceptions (your spouse, a beneficiary less than ten years younger, or a disabled adult child, to name a few), will need to empty the account within ten years of your death.

Also—and this is a pretty big also—check with an attorney if you are considering putting your IRA or 401(k) in a trust. An improperly titled beneficiary form for the IRA could mean the difference of thousands of dollars in taxes. This is just one more reason to work with a financial professional, one who can strategically partner with an estate planning attorney to diligently check your decisions.

CHAPTER 9

Women Retire Too

I help men, women, and families from all walks of life on their journey to and through retirement. Yet, we want to address the female demographic specifically. Why? To be perfectly blunt, women are more likely to deal with poverty than men when they reach retirement.

In 2021, the overall poverty rate for women slightly exceeded the rate for men, but among those seventy-five years and older, 13.51 percent of women lived at the poverty rate compared to 8.82 percent of men.[55]

The topics, products, and strategies I cover elsewhere in this book are meant to help address retirement concerns for men *and* women, but the dire statistic above is a reminder that much of traditional planning is geared toward men. Male careers, male lifespans, male health care. The bottom line is women's career paths often look much different than men's, so why would their retirement planning look the same?

Women often embrace different roles and values than men as workers, wives, mothers, and daughters. They are more apt to take on roles as caretakers. They often plan for events, worry about loved ones, tend to details, and think about the future. Also, they often want everything to be just right, and they want

---

[55] statistica.com. 2023. "Poverty rate in the United States in 2021, by age and gender" https://www.statista.com/statistics/233154/us-poverty-rate-by-gender/

to be right themselves. It could be you've seen the following affixed to a decorative sign, refrigerator magnet, or T-shirt: "If I agreed with you, we'd both be wrong." The barb features a picture of a woman speaking to a man.

If these characteristics I listed about women are accurate, shouldn't they deserve special considerations from financial professionals? The case can be made, particularly since 69 percent of men in the U.S. age sixty-five and older happen to be married, compared to 47 percent of women in that age classification.[56] Single women don't have the opportunity to capitalize on the resource pooling and potential economies of scale accompanying a marriage or partnership.

Women often serve as caretakers for their families. They make sure the people in their lives get places, do things, and function properly. They are also most likely to provide care to anyone in need, including parents who need additional care as they age. In addition, wives tend to live longer than their husbands and may need to provide care for their spouses if the need arises for long-term care.

If the husband indeed passes away first, the wife can sometimes find herself in a situation where no one is around to take care of her. Financial advisors must account for these potential issues by including specific scenarios in retirement plans.

Be Informed

It's a familiar scene in many financial offices across the country: A woman comes into an appointment carrying a sack full of unopened envelopes. Often through tears, she sits across the desk from a financial professional and apologizes her way through a conversation about what financial products she owns and where her income is coming from. She is recently widowed

---

[56] Administration for Community Living. November 30, 2022. "Profile of Older Americans." https://acl.gov/aging-and-disability-in-america/data-and-research/profile-older-americans

and was sure her spouse was taking care of the finances, but now she doesn't know where all their assets are kept, and her confidence in her financial outlook has wavered after walking through funeral expenses and realizing she's down to one income.

Often, she may be financially "okay." Yet, the uncertainty can be wearying, particularly when the family is already reeling from a loss. While this scenario sometimes plays out with men, in my experience, it's more likely to be a woman in that chair across from my desk, probably, in part, because of Western traditions about money management being "a guy thing." But it doesn't have to be this way. This all-too-common scenario can be wiped away with just a little preparation.

Talk to Your Spouse/ Work with a Financial Professional

While there are many factors affecting women's financial preparation for and situation in retirement, I cannot emphasize enough that the decision to be informed, to be a part of the conversation, and to be aware of what is going on with your finances is absolutely paramount to a confident retirement.

With all the couples I've seen, there is almost always an "alpha" when it comes to finances. It isn't always men—for many of my coupled clients, the wife is the alpha who keeps the books and budgets and knows where all of the family's assets are, down to the penny—yet, statistically, among baby boomers it is usually a man who runs the books. But, as time goes on, it looks like the ratio of male to female financial alphas is evening out based on my experience speaking with couples.

The breakdown happens when there is a lack of communication, when no one other than the financial alpha knows how much the family has and where. In the end, it doesn't matter who handles the money; it's about all parties being informed of what's going on financially.

There are a lot of ways to open the conversation about money. One woman started a conversation with her husband, the financial alpha, by sitting down and saying, "Teach me how to be a widow." Perhaps that sounds grim, but it was to the point, and it spurred what she said was a very fruitful conversation.

They spent a day, just one part of an otherwise dull weekend, going through everything she might need to know. They spent the better part of two decades together after that. When he died, and she was widowed, she said the "widowhood" talk had made a huge difference. She knew who to call to talk through their retirement plan and where to call for the insurance policy.

Years later, she accompanied a recently widowed friend of hers to a financial appointment. Her friend was emotional the whole time, afraid she would run out of money any day. The financial professional ultimately showed the friend that she was financially in good shape, but not before the friend had already spent months worried that each check would exhaust her bank account. That's no way to live after losing a loved one. It was preventable had her deceased spouse and financial professional included her in a conversation about "widowhood."

Couples sometimes have their first real conversation about money, assets, and their retirement income approach, in our office. The important thing about having these conversations isn't where, it's when . . . and the best "when" is as soon as possible.

Spouse-Specific Options

One area where it might be especially important to be on the same page between spouses is when it comes to financial products or services that have spousal options. A few that come to mind are pensions and Social Security, although life insurance and annuity policies also have the potential to affect both spouses.

With pensions, taking the worker's life-only option is somewhat attractive—after all, the monthly payment is bigger. However, you and your spouse should discuss your options. When we're talking about both of you, as opposed to just one lifespan, there is an increased likelihood at least one of you will live a long, long time. This means the monthly payout will be less, but it also ensures that, no matter which spouse outlives the other, no one will have to suffer the loss of a needed pension paycheck in his or her later retirement years.

While we covered Social Security options in a different chapter, I think some of the spousal information bears repeating. Particularly, if you worked exclusively inside the home for a significant number of years, you may want to talk about taking your Social Security benefits based on your spouse's work history. After all, Social Security is based on your thirty-five highest-earning years.

Things to remember about the spousal benefits:[57]

- Your benefit will be calculated as a percentage (up to 50 percent) of your spouse's earned monthly benefit at his or her full retirement age, or FRA.

- For you to begin receiving a spousal benefit, your spouse must have already filed for his or her own benefits and you must be at least sixty-two.

- You can qualify for a full half of your spouse's benefits if you wait until you reach FRA to file.

- Beginning your benefits earlier than your FRA will reduce your monthly check but waiting to file until after FRA will not increase your benefits.

For divorcees:[58]

- You may qualify for an ex-spousal benefit if . . .
    a. You were married for a decade or more

---

57 Social Security Administration. "Retirement Planner: Benefits For You As A Spouse." https://www.ssa.gov/planners/retire/applying6.html
58 Social Security Administration. "Retirement Planner: If You Are Divorced." https://www.ssa.gov/planners/retire/divspouse.html

    b. ***and*** you are at least sixty-two

    c. ***and*** you have been divorced for at least two years

    d. ***and*** you are currently unmarried

    e. ***and*** your ex-spouse is sixty-two (qualifies to begin taking Social Security)

- Your ex-spouse does not need to have filed for you to file on his or her benefit.
- Similar to spousal benefits, you can qualify for up to half of your ex-spouse's benefits if you wait to file until your FRA.
- If your ex-spouse dies, you may file to receive a widow/widower benefit on his or her Social Security record as long as you are at least age sixty and fulfill all the other requirements on the preceding alphabetized list.

    a. This will not affect the benefits of your ex-spouse's current spouse

For widow's (or widower's, for that matter) benefits:[59]

- You may qualify to receive as much as your deceased spouse would have received if . . .

    a. You were married for at least nine months before his or her death

    b. ***or*** you would qualify for a divorced spousal benefit

    c. ***and*** you are at least sixty

    d. ***and*** you did not/have not remarried before age sixty

- You may earn delayed credits on your spouse's benefit *if* your spouse hadn't already filed for benefits when he or she died.

---

[59] Social Security Administration. "Survivors Planner: If You Are The Worker's Widow Or Widower."
https://www.ssa.gov/planners/survivors/ifyou.html#h2

- Other rules may apply to you if you are disabled or are caring for a deceased spouse's dependent or disabled child.

Longevity

On average, women live longer than men. Most stats put average female longevity at about two years more than men. But averages are tricky things. An April 2022 report by the World Economic Forum listed the eight oldest people in the world to all be women. They ranged in age from 118 years old to 114 and included two Americans.[60]

On one hand, this is a Brandi Chastain moment. You know, when the American soccer icon shed her jersey to celebrate a game-winning penalty kick to win the World Cup. Seriously, how fabulous are women? They tend to be meticulous, resolute, and perseverant. On the other hand, the trend for women to live longer presents longstanding financial ramifications.

Simply Needing More Money in Retirement

Living longer in retirement means needing more money, period. Barring a huge lottery win or some crazy stock market action, the date you retire is likely the point at which you have the most money you will ever have. Not to put too grim a spin on it, but the problem with longevity is, the further you get away from that date, the further your dollars have to stretch. If you planned to live to a nice eighty-something but live to a nice one-hundred-something, that is *two decades* you will need to account for, monetarily.

To put this in perspective, let's say you like to drink coffee as an everyday splurge. Not accounting for inflation or leap years,

---

[60] Martin Armstrong. World Economic Forum. April 29, 2022. "How old are the world's oldest people?"
https://www.weforum.org/agenda/2022/04/the-oldest-people-in-the-world/

a $2.50 cup-a-day habit is $18,250 over a two-decade span. Now, think of all the things you like to do that cost money. Add those up for twenty years of unanticipated costs. I think you'll see what I mean.

During the 2020 onset of the coronavirus pandemic, many learned to cut costs. For some, that amounted to skipping their decadent latte. For others, however, cutbacks became acute. According to data compiled by Age Wave and Edward Jones, 32 percent of Americans plan to retire later than planned because of the pandemic. Women felt a more adverse effect. The report stipulated that 41 percent of women continued to save for retirement, compared to 58 percent of men.[61]

More Health Care Needs

In addition to the cost of living for a longer lifespan is the fact aging, plain and simple, means more health care, and more health care means more money. Women are survivors. They suffer from the morbidity-mortality paradox, which states women suffer more non-fatal illnesses throughout their lifetime than men, who experience fewer illnesses but higher mortality.

Women have been found to seek treatment more often when not feeling well and emphasize staying healthy when older, according to studies. Survival, I believe, is on the side of the woman. However, surviving things, like cancer, also means more checkups later in life.

A statistical concern for women involves the prospect of long-term care. Long-term care for women lasts 3.7 years on average compared to 2.2 years for men.[62]

---

[61] Megan Leonhardt. cnbc.com. June 16, 2021. "58% of men were able to continue saving for retirement during the pandemic—but only 41% of women were." https://www.cnbc.com/2021/06/16/why-pandemic-hit-womens-retirement-savings-more-than-mens.html

[62] Lindsay Modglin. singlecare.com. February 15, 2022. "Long-term care statistics 2022" https://www.singlecare.com/blog/news/long-term-care-statistics/

Widowhood

Not only do women typically live longer than their same-age male counterparts, they also stand a greater chance of living alone as they age. Some divorce, separate or never marry. Among those age sixty-five and over, 33 percent of women live alone compared to 20 percent of men.[63]

I don't write this to scare people; rather, I think it's fundamentally important to prepare my female clients for something that may be a startling, *but very likely,* scenario. At some point, most women will have to handle their financial situations on their own. A little preparation can go a long way, and having a basic understanding of your household finances and the "who, what, where, and how much" of your family's assets is incredibly useful—it can prevent a tragic situation from being more traumatic.

In my opinion, the financial services industry sometimes underserves women in these situations. Some financial professionals tend to alienate women, even when their spouses are alive. I've heard several stories of women who sat through meeting after meeting without their financial professional ever addressing a single question to them.

In our firm, when we work with couples, we work hard to make sure our retirement income strategies work for *both* people. No matter who the financial alpha is, it's important for everyone affected by a retirement strategy to understand it.

There are times when a couple will come into our office and generally, the man has been the one who has handled the finances and the investments and arguably has done a great job. But at some point, they've had a conversation where she has zero idea about what's going on and realizes if he passes away, she won't know what to do, nor does she know who she can trust. After couples attend one of our seminars, they sometimes

---

[63] statistica.com. November 23, 2022. "Share of senior households living alone in the United States 2020, by gender"
https://www.statista.com/statistics/912400/senior-households-living-alone-usa/

come in wanting to learn more about the strategies discussed during the presentation. . Not necessarily because they think I can do a better job than the husband does, but because they realize that there are additional strategies we may recommend.

But even more important, the wife now has a connection with me, somebody the couple has entrusted to be their financial advisor. It's an obligation I recognize and take seriously.

Hopefully, a couple has vetted four or five different advisors before deciding to work with our company. So, if something happens to the husband, God forbid, the wife has already come in and has a longstanding, trustful relationship with me. She knows we're going to do everything to build a retirement plan that incorporates the needs of both the wife and the husband. They'll hire me because of that desired relationship. It goes back to the importance of developing this kind of relationship just to have somebody to lean on for the man or woman. That connection is huge to me, too, and why I became a financial advisor.

Establishing this relationship early is crucial as there are other risks if the husband passes away before his spouse. The wife now becomes a single filer for income taxes. Also, his passing makes a Roth conversion much more difficult. That's why we want to do it early. Then, obviously, she'll get to retain the highest of their two Social Security benefit streams, but she may lose some income, such as a pension.

Taxes

One of the often-unexpected aspects of widowhood is the tax bill. Many women continue similar lifestyles to the ones they shared with their spouses. This, in turn, means continuing to have a similar need for income. However, after the death of a spouse, their taxes will be calculated based on a single filer's income table, which is much less forgiving than the couple's tax rates. With proper planning, your financial professional and tax advisor may be able to help you take the sting out of your new tax status.

Caregiving

Caregiving.org updates its national report about every five years. According to its findings released in 2020, of the 53 million caregivers providing unpaid, informal care for older adults, 61 percent are women. Among today's family caregivers, 61 percent work and 45 percent report some kind of financial impact from providing a loved one care and support.[64]

In addition to the financial burden created by caregiving responsibilities, women often devote many hours each day to duties such as housekeeping and looking after loved ones. So then, when can women find the time to focus long and hard on financial matters?

Unfortunately, the impact and hardships created by traditional roles for women typically do not account for Social Security benefit losses or the losses of health care benefits and retirement savings. This also doesn't account for maternity care, mothers who homeschool, or women who leave the workforce to care for their children in any way.

I don't repeat these statistics to scare you. Not only are unpaid family caregivers spending their time and energy taking care of others, but they're also putting their own money towards the cause. An AARP study found that three-quarters of family caregivers surveyed were spending an average of $7,242 a year on out-of-pocket caregiving costs.[65] Yet, I think the emotional value of the care many women provide their elderly relatives or neighbors cannot be quantified. So, to be clear, this shouldn't

---

[64] caregiving.org. 2020 Report. "Caregiving in the U.S. 2020."
https://www.caregiving.org/caregiving-in-the-us-2020/
[65] Nancy Kerr. AARP. June 29, 2021. " Family Caregivers Spend More Than $7,200 a Year on Out-of-Pocket Costs."
https://www.aarp.org/caregiving/financial-legal/info-2021/high-out-of-pocket-costs.html

be taken as a "why not to provide caregiving" spiel. Instead, it should be seen as a call for "why to *prepare* for caregiving" or "how to lessen the financial and emotional burden of caregiving."

Funding Your Own Retirement

For these reasons, women need to be prepared to fund more of their own retirements. There are several savings options and products, including the spousal IRA. Unlike a traditional IRA, where you contribute money to a plan with your employer, a spousal IRA is something you or your spouse sets up on your behalf, so he or she can contribute a portion of the paycheck to your retirement funds. This is something to consider, particularly for families where one spouse has dropped out of the workforce to care for a relative.

Also, if you find yourself in a caregiving role, talk to your employer's human resources department. Some companies have paid leave, special circumstances, or sick leave options you could qualify for, making it easier to cope and helping you stay in the workforce longer.

Saving Money

Women need more money to fund their retirements, period. But this doesn't have to be a significant burden—often, women are better at saving, while usually taking less risk in their portfolios.[66] This gives me reason to believe, as women get more involved in their finances, families will continue to be more confident for retirement, both *his* and *hers*.

---

[66] Maurie Backman. The Motley Fool. March 4, 2021. "A Summary of 20 Years of Research and Statistics on Women in Investing." https://www.fool.com/research/women-in-investing-research/

CHAPTER 10

Charity

Wills and testaments, trusts and powers of attorney—these are all pieces of what we often call legacy planning. But I would be remiss if I didn't address a piece of legacy preparation near and dear to my heart: charitable contributions.

Charity is one of those universal concepts that unites us as human beings. Football players who dedicate their resources to building homes for single moms, communities who help neighbors rebuild after catastrophes, groundskeepers who donate millions from under a mattress to their favorite university, or private donors who put impoverished children through school. . .these are the stories that inspire us, that drive us to be better people.

There are many, many ways to pass money to your favorite charity, university, foundation, or public resource. Some include using qualified charitable distributions with the mandatory withdrawals from your IRA, and others lend themselves to establishing trusts. Whatever your preferred method of charitable distribution, the right financial professional will partner with a qualified tax advisor and/or estate planning attorney to discover how to help you make your contributions in a way that fits well within your own strategy for taxes—helping to ensure your contributions are passed efficiently to your intended beneficiary.

Where to Start?

We've all heard it is better to give than to receive, and science backs this up. Multiple studies show those who give to charity or volunteer experience less depression, lower blood pressure, higher self-esteem, and greater happiness.[67]

It's a common perception, however, that retirees are less inclined to be charitable. It seems like reasoned logic—they're living on fixed incomes, and it's difficult to work charitable giving into conservative strategies designed to protect assets. But this counters the facts. In 2021, more baby boomers donated to charities than any other generations.[68]

So, how do we keep up—or even increase—our donations in retirement? Well, as with all the other topics we cover in this book, step one is to build charitable giving into our retirement plans. Advanced planning can help you be sure your donations—at least in the monetary sense—are given in the most tax-efficient and effective way, both for you and for the charity to which you are contributing.

Planned Giving: Lifetime

When we're talking about charitable contributions, it's important to distinguish between lifetime giving and charitable giving as part of a well-prepared estate plan.

The American tax system has many provisions to encourage charitable giving. I'm sure the reasoning goes something along the lines of, if we the people were naturally able, through our own means, to care for the poor and vulnerable in our own communities, we collectively would need to pay fewer taxes to

---

[67] "Volunteering and Its Surprising Benefits."
https://www.helpguide.org/articles/healthy-living/volunteering-and-its-surprising-benefits.htm
[68] Dawn Papandrea. Lendingtree. November 29, 2021. "56% of Americans Donated to Charity in 2021, at Average of $574."
https://www.lendingtree.com/debt-consolidation/charitable-donations-survey-study/

support federal aid to those same people. It's a wonderful consideration, and one we should all aspire to. But, in practice, it gets more difficult, as tax codes change and shift according to political administrations and other public considerations. Ensuring your charitable contributions are tax-efficient is not a one-time move—it requires yearly analysis.

It's important to remember your charitable giving is most effective when the combined amount of your *itemized* deductions is more than your *standard* deduction. Now it isn't only charity that counts toward your itemized deduction; there are also homeowner and business owner credits, adoption credits, etc. But, as it pertains to charity, if you haven't contributed a significant amount to charity in a certain tax year, it may not be worth counting on your taxes.

Deductions change year-to-year, of course, but the IRS usually publishes the following year's charts in November. When you're itemizing deductions, you may deduct up to 50 percent of your adjusted gross (pre-tax) income, though in some cases, 20 percent and 30 percent limitations apply.[69]

Another thing to keep in mind if you are considering the tax implications of a charitable donation, you must have a receipt, a canceled check, or some demonstrable way of recording the transaction. Additionally, many charitable activities aren't eligible for tax credits. Raffle tickets, charity event entrance fees, and those sorts of things are not typically counted as charitable deductions on your taxes—a quick rule of thumb is, if you received something in return for your donation, it's not tax-deductible.

Perhaps one of the most crucial things to keep in mind when it comes to the tax implications of charitable giving, however, is "nonprofit" doesn't mean "tax advantaged." The IRS keeps a long list of organizations that qualify for tax-deducted gifting in the Internal Revenue Code section 501(c)(3). Yet, many

---

[69] IRS.gov. August 25, 2022. "Charitable Contribution Deductions" https://www.irs.gov/charities-non-profits/charitable-organizations/charitable-contribution-deductions#.

excellent nonprofits and civic organizations are not 501(c)(3)s. That doesn't mean you shouldn't give to them—truly, charity is *not* about tax deductions when it comes right down to it—it just means you shouldn't plan to include it as part of your tax-efficiency strategies.

Again, I would be remiss to not emphasize that these laws and definitions change year to year, so it is important to work with a team of qualified financial and tax professionals who can help you plan for the future and adjust to the times, in addition to verifying whether the charity you are considering is tax-exempt.

While impermanence seems to be a fixture of our tax system, one important aspect of charity tax law was made permanent for the foreseeable future. In 2015, Congress passed a budget deal signed into law by President Barack Obama. Among the provisions of the "Protecting Americans From Tax Hikes Act of 2015," which included this important measure::

> IRA charitable rollovers — at age seventy-and-one-half, owners of traditional IRAs can make direct gifts of up to $100,000 a year to a qualified charity directly from the IRA.[70] This is known as a qualified charitable distribution or QCD.

What makes permanent deduction No. 3 so important is a person who uses an IRA to contribute to charity in this way can: 1. Be charitable, 2. Avoid having their RMDs push them into a higher tax bracket by instead gifting them to those in need, 3. Take advantage of the tax-free aspect of a QCD when planning charitable gifting, and 4. Potentially use the tax break to offset other tax consequences, like the tax on appreciated assets or capital gains. With an allowance for IRA contributions after an individual reaches age seventy-three, QCDs will be adversely affected if a contribution is made to that IRA in the same year a QCD is withdrawn.

------

[70] Council on Foundations. 2022. "IRA Charitable Rollover" https://www.cof.org/content/ira-charitable-rollover-0#

When it comes to charitable giving, we'll talk to clients about a couple of things. The first one is part of our financial planning guide, the document prospective clients fill out prior to our first meeting in the office. We ask if they contribute to a charity, and, if so, how much, and which ones are near and dear to their hearts. Frequently, they'll mention a church, but sometimes they give a lot of money to a charity because an impactful event inspired them to give to that organization.

We find that many of our clients give to charity because it means something special to them, not because of any tax break they may gain. Giving, however, can trigger a favorable tax event if done correctly. For our clients who do not want to face an additional tax increase from required minimum distributions, the QCD can be an invaluable tool. The use of a QCD can offset potential tax implications caused by the required withdrawal from an IRA account.

Planned Giving: After My Lifetime

For many charities, endowments and legacy gifts are the lifeblood that keeps them going. And, for many of us, a large final gift is an excellent way to continue a legacy of giving into perpetuity. The financial reasons for final charitable gifts, much like the annual contributions we often give, are many and, mostly, tax-based. A large final gift can be a good way to offload highly appreciated assets, allowing our favorite charities to experience the full use of an asset without us having to pay out a sizable tax bill.

Many charities have gone to great lengths to make this an attractive option, with some having preferences for certain donation types and strategies. For instance, many public entities, such as libraries and schools, have foundations to collect most of the donations and do major fundraising. Churches and universities often have special projects and intentional funding that stems from sizable endowments.

There are many financial vehicles to help you meet your charitable goals and give you benefits during your lifetime as well—from permanent life insurance policies to charitable trusts and charitable annuities. That's why it's important to plan ahead and work with a goal in mind. If you have some idea of what end you want to achieve, it can be easier to find the estate attorneys, tax professionals, and financial professionals who will be best qualified to help.

Non-Monetary Charitable Contributions

Ultimately, aside from the tax breaks, the good feeling, and the name on a park bench you might receive, your charitable contributions aren't about what you "get" in return. This is one other reason we should plan ahead for our good works; it's about doing the right thing.

Volunteering is one great, non-monetary way to support the charities and causes we believe in. Like I noted earlier, research shows retirees who are active and engaged volunteers in their communities often have a better sense of purpose and report more happiness than those who aren't. In volunteering, we have a reason to get up in the morning, and we meet new people and make friends. These are all things that may previously have stemmed from your nine-to-five workday but tend to fall by the wayside after leaving the workforce, making this consideration even more important.

As a firm, we pick out two charities each year and either do some type of fundraising drive for the charity or donate money directly to the charity. We once had a drive for K9s for Warriors. Clients donated materials for the soldiers and the dogs. We also work with a local organization called Hart Felt Ministries. I served on its board of directors for nine years. The charity assists older citizens to help them stay in their homes longer.

It's important to our firm to be philanthropic and to give back to the community that gives to us. On our website, we list the events and organizations we support. When we work with small local charities, we find we can make a big impact, and these are often the same charities our clients are already giving to.

We also ask our clients if they are on the board of a specific charity and attempt to get involved with those charities. Also, we aspire to maintain a patriotic theme in our office, giving back to those who sacrifice for us. So, again, we've enjoyed working with organizations like K9s for Warriors and Folds of Honor.

Our families are one way we leave a legacy. But charitable giving—with our time, our talents, and our treasure—allows us to extend our legacies even further, beyond passing on Grandpa's nose or Grandma's ticklish feet.

CHAPTER 11

Finding a Financial Professional

During the most recent expansion of our NuVenture Financial Group office space, we created a motivational wall. The artwork contains messages every member of the team uses as inspiration each day. The phrases reflect a mix of scripture, quotes, and axioms anyone can read for encouragement.

My favorite is in the middle and is drawn from a financial advisor named Joel Johnson, whose presentations I have attended regularly. Joel insists advisors change lives; I'm convinced too. Our work helping clients establish income plans while identifying other retirement needs can prove instrumental.

As a team, we take that to heart. When we huddle to begin each work week to discuss what is happening at our office, we close by putting our hands in the middle and in unison shout, "Change Lives!"

We don't charge out the door ready to apply a full-court press or quarterback blitz, but the team mindset is fully engaged in a belief we wholeheartedly share.

Let's retrace the steps I took after abruptly leaving the banking industry upon reading an email detailing my termination. I decided to take another position in financial services selling life insurance. My livelihood depended on commissions, which is not comforting when trying to build a book of business from scratch and also providing for a family.

Yet that wasn't all that I struggled with. I learned I could not help client families to the extent I wanted by only providing insurance products. I also didn't want to obtain a securities license just to work with clients at growing their investment portfolios.

My designation is RICP®, which stands for Retirement Income Certified Professional. When I sought to further distinguish myself in the financial services industry, I looked into many different certifications and designations. They almost amount to an alphabet soup of titles that those in our industry can possess.

Each denotes its own specialty. I'm a retirement planner. Our team devotes its energy and passion to this financial realm. Retirement planning is what we do every day. We believe it to be a noble pursuit, and RICP® ideally reflects my holistic approach to retirement planning.

That approach takes consumers through the many considerations they could face in retirement. Retirement plans we devise include income and investment planning, yet also account for other key factors such as Social Security, legacy and estate planning, tax efficiency, insurance, and health care.

Comprehensive Retirement Plan

Before even touching on those aspects, however, our staff stresses the importance of identifying your purpose in retirement. While lounging in an easy chair sounds better than punching your alarm clock and reporting for work, it can be easy to get bored when you have idle time to fill. Travel aspirations, family visits, hobbies, and lifestyle choices should be top of mind—elements to consider when developing your retirement budget.

Frankly, it's not just our staff changing lives. Clients find they also undergo life changes as their spirit takes them on different adventures in retirement.

I'll never forget a comment from an eventual client immediately after she stepped into our office for the first time:

"I feel like retirement is like having to walk up to the edge of a steep cliff . . . knowing I have to step off."

Retirement made her feel uneasy. The life she spent consisted of solid ground fortified by paychecks she received while spending thirty-plus years in the workforce. But the cliff represented a new beginning. She knew she would have to step off and confront her new reality. Would she be okay? And if so, what would her retirement lifestyle look like? It is the reason she scheduled an appointment and visited me.

Again, retirement is more than just an investment. The problem is many people, including some financial professionals, equate retirement to an investment or rate of return. Money is merely a tool to help achieve your goals and should never be the primary focus for enjoying a successful and rewarding retirement.

NuVenture Financial Group is much more interested in forging relationships with our client families than learning how much wealth they have accumulated. I believe this is the path to building a sustainable financial planning business, which I enjoy working for and owning.

Over time my team developed, refined, and trademarked a five-step process we use when we begin working with a new family. We refer to it as the Retirement in Perspective™ process—or RP5.

Step 1: Picture

This is our first meeting, and that's literally all we're doing—getting a good picture of each other. It's something like a first date. Do I like you, and do you like me? The first half of this ninety-minute meeting is where I review the questionnaire they completed before the visit.

What are their goals and ambitions? Essentially, what do they want their retirement to look like? What does their "perfect day" in retirement look like? About halfway through the meeting, I begin to tell them more about me and my firm. I go into who we are, our philosophies, our financial planning process, how we help our current clients, and what their experience looks like.

Step 2: Stress Test

At the end of the first visit, we decide if it's a good idea to get back together for a second one. I tease people and tell them not to worry—we don't have an EKG machine or treadmill in the back of our office. It's not that kind of stress test; it's a financial stress test encompassing my professional observations. Basically, if I was them—but knowing what I know as a retirement planner, having done this hundreds of times—what would I be paying attention to? What are the things I would be addressing?

I try to put myself in their shoes and address items I find important. These are my observations regarding factors we need to cover and potentially address. I will also explain the three categories of money and savings. We review some of the software packages we use to assist us in our planning, we have a comprehensive discussion on fees and compensation, and I answer any remaining questions they may have. The main objective of this second meeting is for them to get as much value as possible from their appointment. This is crucial because at the end of this meeting, we'll discuss if we both want to continue moving forward.

Step 3: Design

If we decide we're the right fit for each other, we enter the third step, which we call the Design stage. Unlike the first two steps, the Design stage may require two or three meetings, depending on the complexity of the design. Both parties mutually agree to a design each of us likes. Typically, the families I work with want straightforward strategies, not complex investment products that are vague and hard to understand. So, "simple" is what I attempt to deliver to them. I've found over time that those I work with are smart, successful people capable of making appropriate decisions.

However, what I know they typically lack is unbiased information to be able to make those decisions. This is what I try to deliver—sound advice. Once I've given them the information they need, their opinion may be different than mine—and that's okay. As long as I've delivered what I believe are sound pieces of information, options, and recommendations to them, they can make their own decisions on the best way to tackle the problem.

Step 4: Build

Much like building a new home, you first must design it before you build it. In this step, we're transferring money to different accounts and ultimately to their final destination to set the plan in motion.

Step 5: Guide

We enter the Guide stage once the customized retirement plan has been established. We begin and maintain a relationship with our client families. Life throws curveballs at us, and they don't stop in retirement. Our job as retirement planners is to position the plan and our firm to be there when that time comes. Communication and relationships are key, and very often, we see clients five to six times per year in meetings and events.

Among them:

- Annual strategic and tactical planning meetings
- "Focus" meetings that last one hour and address specific topics such as tax planning, Medicare, Social Security, and other considerations
- Quarterly "Lunch and Learn" sessions
- Semi-annual client appreciation events

The first four steps in this process are designed to get new clients on track. Step Five is designed to *keep* them on track. Our RP5™ process is considered unique by some, especially those who tell us their initial experience and first meeting with a broker at a different company sound like a sales pitch.

This is why some are apprehensive about meeting with us for the first time. I don't blame them. They're leery of another sales pitch. However, I believe we're different because we're much more interested in taking our time to make sure a relationship with a prospective client is the right fit.

We're building our firm on high-quality relationships with clients rather than a vast quantity of clients. I want to make sure we get it right rather than get it done quickly.

Fees

In recent years, advertising in your local newspaper has diminished. So too has the size of the paper. More people are accustomed to reading news online, or look for other sources, including those without a paywall. Advertisers don't find as much value in placing ads in the actual print version of the paper. Declines in circulation are primarily to blame. Also, many former advertisers have company websites, which they use to drive consumer traffic.

However, if you happen to be someone who receives the newspaper in your driveway, you might have noticed that grocery store circulars are still a thing. Sure, the circulars might be a bit smaller. Yet, grocers still see some advantages to listing numerous prices for sales items in print, which readers can often scan much easier than looking up individual items on a website.

Those newspaper ads continue to be printed as a service to consumers. They want to see prices—in some cases before they ever step into the store—so they can prepare their shopping lists accordingly.

Why then should the cost of doing business with a financial professional often seem like a clandestine mystery? Well, to be blunt, it shouldn't. Consumers should know how much it will cost them to work with a financial professional and how exactly they arrive at the fees charged.

Now, fees can be troublesome. You can't get something for nothing, and fees are how many financial companies and professionals make a living. Yet, it's important to recognize even a fee of a single percentage point is money out of your pocket—money that represents not just the one-time fee of today but also represents an opportunity cost. For someone approaching retirement, how much do you think fees may have cost them over their lifetime?

It is important to look at management fees and assess if you think you're getting what you pay for. Here's an example:

Assume you're 40 years old and plan to retire at age seventy. Your current 401(k) balance is $100,000 (that's right in line with the average balance by age), and you plan to contribute $10,000 each year—about half the allowable amount. Finally, for this example, the assumed investment return (before fees) is 8 percent.

If you pay 0.5 percent in fees, you will have $1,909,490 in your account when you retire. However, if you pay 1 percent in fees, you'll have $1,705,833—or $203,656 less. A calculator at 401kfee.com shows you would have to contribute $2,156 more each year (for three decades) to accumulate the same amount at retirement if you paid 1 percent instead of the lower 0.5 percent fee.

Make sure your advisor is on the same side of the table as you. I suggest you consider working with a fee-based advisor. A purely fee-only advisor cannot sell life insurance, annuities, long-term care solutions, Medicare products, or health insurance. All of these are important items to consider in retirement, and they all pay a commission. By definition, a fee-only advisor typically cannot sell you all available options. I believe that your investments should be fee-only.

An understanding of fees must require context. The fees should be based on the value of services provided and should not reflect just a flat rate without detailing what goes into establishing the fees. If I had a car I wanted to sell for $10,000, the buyer would clearly want to know what it is I'm selling. If it's a Lamborghini that is in good order, the car wouldn't last long in my driveway for that price. If it's a used and bruised Pontiac that looks destined for the junkyard, people would quickly balk at the price. The car sale is all about the value you're getting for the price you're paying.

When someone asks about our fees, I usually respond with another question: "Are you looking for the cheapest fees or the most value?" By focusing on value, we can help ensure that the fees you pay are justified.

If you're looking for an advisor with the lowest fees, then we're probably not a good fit for you. But if you're looking for more value, then we may be a good fit for you. Our advisory fees for assets under management start at 1.5 percent and could decrease based on the amount you have under management.

Acknowledgments

This book would not have been possible without the help and guidance of the following people and more:

Critical in my journey of becoming a successful advisor and business owner, I'd like to thank Bill Aldrich for teaching me how to **survive** in this business, everyone at the Detlef's firm for teaching me how to **thrive** in this business, and Tad Hill for teaching me how to **change lives** in this business.

I would also like to thank:

- My team in Topeka, Kansas . . . Advisors Excel. Thank you for investing your resources in me and my firm. You've seen me grow from a fresh-faced new advisor into the business owner of one of the premier retirement planning firms in Jacksonville.

- Kevin Haskin. Thank you for taking my simple words and sculpting them into a unique song. I appreciate you keeping me accountable and motivated to finish this book.

- My team at NuVenture Financial Group. Because of all of you, I get to observe first-hand many people enjoying their retirements and everything they've worked for their entire lives. All of you and your hard work truly make that possible. Never forget that.

- Chris Morrison and Jenna Lolly. You've been critical in making NuVenture what it is today and what it is to become. I can't thank you both enough for your dedication, sacrifice, and hard work.

- Our "NuVenture Families.". Thank you for putting your trust in us. You've literally given us the unique opportunity to help guide you and build on the successes you've created. I will never take those relationships for granted.

- My mom. You've always been my biggest fan and believed in me when it was difficult to do so. You're my inspiration to be better than I ever thought I could be, and you've been a role model of how to treat others. You taught me hope and how to look for the best in difficult situations.

- My four daughters, Alex, Ashlyn, Autumn, and Ansley. Thank you for giving me the ambition to always push for something better and allowing me to be a role model in your life. Because of you four, I've always had the motivation to get up when I've been knocked down.

- My wife and best friend, April. You are my rock. You've been with me in my lowest lows and my highest highs. . .literally at my worst and my best. Thank you for believing in me and always giving me a different perspective when dealing with difficult situations. God truly placed you in my life knowing I need you. I love you always.

About the Author

BOB HORNE, RICP®
CEO/President/Financial Advisor
NuVenture Financial Group

Bob's goal is to empower clients to make informed decisions and help achieve their retirement goals.

After entering the financial services industry, Bob served as an assistant vice president and branch manager for HSBC Bank. In an effort to find a professional atmosphere that matched his own commitment to building client relationships, Bob made a career change to specifically focus on retirement strategies. After working as a financial professional with two local Jacksonville firms for seven years, he decided to pursue his entrepreneurial vision and launched NuVenture Financial

Group in 2019. As the CEO of NuVenture, Bob uses his passion for problem-solving to help individuals and families with their long-term retirement strategies.

Bob has passed the Series 6, 63, and 65 securities exams and carries a life, health, and annuity license in Florida. He has also obtained the industry-leading Retirement Income Certified Professional® (RICP®) designation.

Bob resides in Mandarin, Florida, with his wife, April, and four daughters, Alex, Ashlyn, Autumn, and Ansley. In his spare time, he enjoys being outdoors and spending time with his family.

Additionally, Bob is actively involved with his church. . For nine years, he formerly served as the treasurer on the board of directors with the local nonprofit organization, Hart Felt Ministries. He is a founding member and past president of both the Capital Gain Chapter of Business Networking International (BNI) and Core Network Referral Group (CNRG).

JACKSONVILLE
13241 Bartram Park Blvd., Suite 913
Jacksonville, FL 32258

Phone: 904.253.7600
Email: info@nuventurefinancialgroup.com
Website: nuventurefinancialgroup.com